RASTRICK – THEN AND NOW

Researched and written by
MARGARET USHER

Margaret Usher March 18th 2013

Modern photography by
BOB DUNN

Published 2012 by
Margaret Usher

ISBN
978-0-9574770-0-1

Page Layout by Highlight Type Bureau Ltd, Bradford BD8 7HB

Printed by The Amadeus Press, Cleckheaton BD19 4TQ

CONTENTS

ACKNOWLEDGEMENTS

We are grateful to the National Archives for permission to use information found in the Census records for Rastrick and to the West Yorkshire Archives for permission to use some of their photographs, especially those in the Roy Brooks Collection (ref: WYK1450/2/) and two pertaining to Bridge End Independent Chapel in the Kirklees section of the WYAS. They also gave us permission to use a parish marriage certificate. The inventories mentioned in some of the public houses are also among their records. The Brighouse Echo has been most helpful too, allowing us access to, and permission to use, material from their Archives. We are grateful to A. H. Leach and in particular, John Leach, for permission to use the photos of various branches of the Brighouse & District Cooperative Society. Our thanks go to the Reverend Matthew Pollard for his help in giving us access to the interiors of both the Church of St. John the Divine and St. Matthew's Church and also to the photographs showing the construction of the former. We are grateful for the technical information given in Roy Brooks' excellent books on the history of Huddersfield trams.

We are grateful to Charles Squire and Derek Rawlinson for photos from their collections and the many inhabitants of Rastrick who have produced old photos and memories which have been most helpful and informative. The proprietor of Lands House allowed us to photograph aspects of the interior which has allowed us a glimpse of Victorian ornamentation and the modern technology of their day.

The advice and help given by Amadeus Press has been most encouraging and the author in particular is most grateful to them.

INTRODUCTION

Rastrick Library is celebrating its Centenary this year and over two years ago the Rastrick Local History Group was launched to research into the History of the village. The old photographs in this book formed one of the starting points in the early stages of our research. It was felt that we should take photographs of the same places and buildings and compare them. This book grew out of that. We have limited it to those comparison photographs although as you go through the book, you will see that some subjects have more examples of old scenes than others.

The modern photographs were taken between July 2011 and September 2012.

It is not meant to be a definitive book but one which provokes memories and perhaps will persuade everyone to look in their attics, cellars and hidey-holes for more photos that they would be willing to share with the Rastrick Local History Group.

During the last two years we have been researching on the deeper side of the history of Rastrick and intend to publish our findings.

In the meantime, please enjoy this and let us know any facts you could add!

November 2012

Rastrick Library Centenary 1912-2012

In 2009 this Listed Building was repaired and restored/refurbished.

Bridge End

In the early census records, some enumerators called this area "Salford".

Bridge End in 1915 with Mason's Butchers and the railway arches in the background

The Star Inn is on the right of this photograph taken in 1915, the building beyond the Star Inn and nearer the railway bridge, is the White Lion pub which didn't compete well with the Duke of York Inn, the Star Inn and the Rising Sun in close proximity. It was demolished many years ago and since 2003 a large house has been built with a well laid out terraced garden on that land. The shops on the left in this photo included Mason's the Butcher's shop and the block of houses behind had a small shop (not visible in this photo) on the corner of Scotty Bank with the door opening literally on to the corner. The area where the young girl is walking towards the shops on the original photograph was in front of the Rising Sun pub. This pub faced the Star Inn which had probably been a coaching inn.

Modern junction of Bridge End and Bramston Street

The Star Inn in 2011 The butchers shop is still there but no longer a butcher's.

Nowadays, those shops have lost their shades and the nearest one is no longer a butcher's. At the time this photo was taken in 2011, it was a mortgage lender's office.

Bridge End looking up towards Rastrick Common.

Another view of Bridge End shows the White Lion on the left with the Star beyond it. Beyond the shops on the right is the Rising Sun. Bridge End goes up towards Rastrick Common.

Bridge End in 2012 looking up towards Rastrick Common

The Duke of York Inn, Bridge End, Rastrick.

In 1834 this pub was run by Mercy Webster, who later had brewing premises and stables nearer the railway station. In 1845 Abraham Holt was the innkeeper[1] By 1861 the landlord was William Brook, who combined being the landlord with being a Flock Dealer. In 1863 William Sutcliffe had taken over the pub and ran it until he moved to the Upper George in 1878.

In 1881 the pub was in the hands of Jonathan Fielding and his wife Ann. Jonathan had been a worsted singer[2] in Northowram before taking on the pub. He died on 21st November 1886 and his executors were granted Probate of his Will in December 1886. His personal effects were valued at £258 9s 6d. His widow, Ann, took over the pub and was running it in 1891. She was followed by Samuel N. Eastwood in 1897 and he was there in the 1901 Census. He continued as landlord for several years after this.

In the early years of the 20th Century several volunteer Rifle Clubs were formed following the end of the Boer War. In 1907 this pub was a member of the Brighouse & District Licensed Victuallers Air Gun and Rifle League along with several more pubs in Rastrick.

Duke of York Inn from under the Railway arch

[1] Walker's Trade Directory 1845

[2] He was not a worsted chorister but a skilled worker who singed the cloth to remove unwanted 'hairs'.

Where the Duke of York Inn stood is now a taxi rank

By 1909 Henry Wallace Evans was the Licensee. Before entering the Licensing Trade, Henry had been a boiler maker in Halifax. He died on 18 August that year. His widow was granted probate on 2 September 1909. He left personal effects of £225 16s 10d. His wife took over the pub.

In 1911 Jane Evans, Henry's widow, aged 49 years was still the Licensee. Her daughters Margarita aged 19 years and Clarice aged 14 years assisted her. That Census described the Inn as having 11 rooms. How long she remained there is not clear but on 31 Oct 1919 James Bond became landlord and was there until 1927. When he left the magistrates closed the pub and in 1933 it was demolished for road widening.

In 1922 one of the shops on the other side of the road from the Duke of York Inn was a fruiterer's owned by Herbert King who had taken it over from a Mr. Murray. Later it was inherited by Herbert's son, Eric. The premises next to that were, at some time, a shoe repair business run by Mr. Lightowler and next to that was Mr. Rhodes the confectioner. Next to that was a butcher's shop which was owned at some point by Mr. Gilbert Sowden. That shop later became a fishmonger's.

In 2012 those same shops are The Bridge End Diner and City Link, a taxi firm. They have both been enlarged to take in more than a single shop area.

Demolition of the pub in 1933.

The pub has gone but where is the widening of the road?

Looking at the photographs one has to ask oneself just how much road widening there has been or was it the junction with Cliffe Road that was altered?

The Star Inn, Bridge End

There has been a pub on this site for about 300 years. It had stabling for horses and provided accommodation. It also brewed its own beer as many pubs did during that time. In the cellars of this pub there are the remnants of the brewing equipment.

Was this old brewing equipment

or a boiler for heating water?

a fire can be lit below

looking into the top

and what went on here?

1834 – James Marsden
1841 – William Lord.
1851 – William Lord. His Mother, Betty Lord, lived with them and is described as a retired innkeeper.
1861 – Caroline Lord widow of William Lord.
1871 – John Exley Dyson (married to William and Caroline's daughter, Hannah.)
1881 – John Exley Dyson who was also a builder and in partnership with James Dyson who also ran the George Hotel in Commercial Street, Brighouse. John's daughter married James' son, who was a retail chemist, in Lancashire after her father died.
1885 - Village Pride Lodge of Oddfellows Manchester Unity met in the pub and enjoyed a substantial dinner.
23rd. January 1886 - The Annual Dinner of the Gladstone Lodge was held at The Star, Bridge End, Rastrick where John Exley Dyson was the landlord.. The company later adjourned to the Club house. There they held the business part of the evening. The Balance sheet having been approved the evening continued with entertainment by 6 Singers:- Messrs P. Rushworth, W. Walton, A. Sykes, W. Sharp, C. East and N. Sharpe and by a recitation by Brother W. Greenwood.
27th January 1886 – Sale by Auction of Leasehold Property in Rastrick. 12 cottages in Rosemary Lane were sold on lease at a yearly ground rent of £3 2s. 2d. they were bought by Mr. Joah Brook of Rastrick for £690.
1891 - John Exley and Hannah Dyson continued to run the pub.
1894 – Brighouse & Rastrick Naturalists Society met here. In 1898 the meetings and the Collection of stuffed birds and exhibits were transferred to the Rydings.
John Exley Dyson was still the licensee in 1897 but soon after he and his family retired to St.Anne's on Sea, Lancashire. There John died on 22 April 1909. His Will named his son, William Lord Dyson, brassfounder, his daughter Emma, spinster, and his son-in-law Herbert Greenwood, bank manager, as his executors. He left £7,564 13s 1d.
Another lasting memento is that his name, in gilt letters, is still displayed above the main entrance to the pub, declaring that John Exley Dyson is licensed to sell Ale, Porter, Wines, Spirits and Tobacco.
John Exley Dyson also re-built part of the pub.

1901 – **Harry Kirby** and Annie E. Kirby.
1906 – Wm. H. Stansfield[3]
1907 – This pub was a member of the **Brighouse & District Licensed Victuallers Air Gun and Rifle League.**
1908 – **Jim Bottomley** became the licensee. He was the son of Edwin and Ann Grace Bottomley who ran the Black Horse Inn on New Hey Road at the top of Rastrick. He married Edith Alice Cupitt in Attercliffe cum Darnall in 1894 and they had one son called Walter who was born in 1895.
1911 – **Jim Bottomley** was running the Star in April at the time of the census but seems to have taken over the Black Horse Inn when his mother died in the Autumn. The Star had eleven rooms.
1912 – Thomas Robinson
1917 – A.A. Fearnside
1921 – James Newsome
1933 – 1939 Tom Fearnley. Before he took over as licensee, Tom had had a bad accident at work as a result of which he had to change jobs. He married Hetty Garfitt, widow of Fred Garfitt, in 1925. Hetty's daughter Edith Alice Garfitt was brought up in the Star Inn until she married Wilfred Seedhouse.
Their daughter's daughter remembers stories her grandmother told her about her childhood, especially tales of her creeping out of bed to look down at the customers from a 'hidey-hole' at the top of the stairs.
2010 – **Sam Keating**
This pub is currently owned by Clifton Properties.

The new road junction dawned where the Rising Sun set

[3] Names of licensees in italics throughout this book mean that the author has not been able to confirm them.

The Rising Sun, 22, Bridge End

The back of the Rising Sun Inn, which faced the Star Inn just visible through the alley way

This photo was taken shortly before the building was demolished. It faced The Star Inn which was a much busier pub with a variety of social events held there. The Star Inn can be seen through the alley way between the Rising Sun and what used to be part of the Bridge End Independent Chapel's manse and old Sunday School. This is now the Bridge End Nursery and Out of School Club.

Mary Schofield is recorded in the area as being an innkeeper but the census does not name the pub. Her son William, aged 19 years, is also identified as being an innkeeper.

1851 census records show Thomas Crowther is a brewer in this area but not where he did the brewing. At that time most innkeepers brewed their own beer.

1871 – **William Curtis** was the beerhouse keeper. He, his wife Hannah and his mother, also called Hannah, lived there and there were two pianists lodging there – Prosper Gallet, aged 25, born in France and John Walker, 49, from Canterbury. William died in the first quarter of 1881. After William's death, Hannah continued as innkeeper and in 1891 she was innkeeper at the Woolpack, Woolshops Yard, Halifax.

1891 – **Edwin Thornton and Ann Thornton**. Edwin was a stone mason.

1901 – John W. Weatherhead

1907 – This pub was a member of the Brighouse & District Licensed Victuallers Air Gun and Rifle League.

1908 – **H. Womersley.** This was possibly the same Harry Womersley who, in 1911, was running the Vulcan Inn in Foundry Street, Rastrick. In 1908 the Council had

The Rising Sun in its Dying Rays in 1913

been wanting to improve the Bramston Street area and had offered Webster's Brewery £640 for it but the offer was rejected. In 1913 Webster's Brewery approached the Brighouse Town Council to inform them they had someone interested in buying the Rising Sun pub. The Highways Committee decided on 22 Jan 1913 to offer the same amount again which Webster's accepted, provided the Council paid the legal transfer costs of £9 12shillings as well. When the sale was completed, the council asked for tenders to be submitted for its demolition which had to be completed within 6 weeks of the day it was started. J. Briggs & Sons were successful. The Highways Committee also decided that the demolished stone would be used to rebuild the boundary wall for the outfall section at Cooper Bridge Sewage works. The Highways Committee improved the road junction and, incidentally, the aspect from the Star Inn.

The new junction seen from the Star Inn

Scotty Bank

J. Horsfall Turner, writing in 1878 has suggested that the name of this road came from a Scotsman who was a clergyman at Bridge End Church because he had a small Croft and a well there. The clergyman he referred to was the Rev. Meldrum who came to Rastrick to be the Minister at Bridge End Independent Chapel in 1785 having been a Minister in Malton for about ten years. Perhaps Rastrick did not appeal to the Rev. Meldrum as he arrived during 1785 and by January 1786 he had preached three times at Hathelow, Cheshire and spent some considerable part of those few months preaching at other Churches, raising funds for Bridge End Church. He left Rastrick in 1786 to take up the Living in Hathelow which suited him better as he stayed there for twenty-eight years. Scotty Bank is still there and also a small passageway called Scotty Croft, but one has to ask oneself if the local populace would have named the croft and well after a man they'd known only six or seven months?

27 November 1948 – A Gas Leak. Just after 4.00 am, Mrs Price at 9, Scotty Bank awoke and smelt gas. She tried to wake her husband but couldn't. She went outside for help but collapsed in the street where a passer-by helped her to her neighbours, Mr. and Mrs. Waddington. They had also woken because of the smell. They went to find Mr. Price who had collapsed behind his own door. The leak was reported and it was found to be from a 6 inch main outside numbers 5, 7 and 9 Scotty Bank, Rastrick, which was reported at 4.30 am and the Gas Department attended to it. They had a very lucky escape.

Scotty Bank circa 1920

Taken from the same viewpoint showing the diverted Scotty Bank in 2011

March 1961 and a Woollen District bus is turning into Scotty Bank

The original start to Scotty Bank now showing how it had been diverted between 1961 and 2011

March 1961 - The original Scotty Bank seen here was steep and narrow with houses on one side and the railway embankment built in 1841-2 on the other. Nevertheless a Yorkshire Woollen District bus regularly turned into it and the two women watching it have great faith in the driver's ability to miss them! Since then most of the houses have been demolished which has allowed the road to be widened and diverted to join Bramston Street just before its junction with Bridge End, making it much safer. The new photo was taken in July 2011. The shop is now a Take-Away.

The boot and shoemaker's shop under the Arches at Bridge End.
The bottom of Scotty Bank is just visible

On the corner underneath the Arches was a clogger's shop. The owner was a well-known local character with a good reputation for mending shoes, boots and clogs. His window was covered with wooden shutters when the shop was closed. He must have been one of the pioneers of "Shoes repaired while you wait" as he often replaced the irons while his customers relaxed and chatted………… which was probably a better option than walking home barefoot! The whole shop has been demolished.

Modern trucks, venturing down here from the motorway, are confronted with a warning sign as the bridge is low. The Arch is now embellished with black and yellow warning chevrons.

The boot and shoemaker's shop has gone

Lillands Farm, Lillands Lane, Rastrick

A Sketch of Lillands Farm, Rastrick[4]

This is one of the oldest houses in Rastrick. There is a datestone on 1741 on one section of the building but inside the house is a section dating from the 16th century with distinctive architectural features from that period.

Over successive centuries, owners have added the modern architectural features of their times, so there are examples of late 18th and early and late 19th century fashion.

Lillands Farm, Rastrick in 2011

[4] Reproduced by permission of the owner in 2011.

Cliffe Road, Rastrick

Cliffe Road showing an entrance to Cliffe House on the left

The houses on the right in the photo taken in 1931 have now been demolished and the grounds of Cliffe House stand above the high wall to the left of the lane. A hundred years ago it was the home of J.W. Miller, founder of Millers' Oils. The access gateway has been blocked up as you can see in the 2011 photo. Cliffe House is now Cliff Hall Club House.

Cliffe Road: the old houses have gone and the entrance way to Cliffe House has been bricked up

Cliff Hall Club

Front of Cliff Hall Club

Front door of Cliff Hall Club

Bridge End Independent Chapel.

At first the members met in various houses but when sufficient members had joined, they decided to build a proper Chapel.

1778 – The first Chapel building was started in this year but by the time they had laid the foundations and built a wall to a height of one yard, money and materials had run out.

1779 Mrs. Morton of Slead Syke encouraged them to plan better so they drew up proper plans and worked out the cost more carefully and built the first Chapel.

The first building was a modest one, comprising a Chapel and school room. Together they could accommodate 300 people. This Chapel was built on land that had been leased for 99 years in 1728 to James Whitaker, a blacksmith, by the Duke of Leeds, the Rt. Hon. Peregrine, Lord Osborne, Marquess of Carmarthen and Lord of the Manor of Wakefield. Apparently, so the story goes, James Whitaker had rendered some considerable service to the Duke of Leeds. Asked what he would like as a reward for this service, he requested the lease of this land next to his existing forge at Bridge End. This was granted and the annual rent was 6d per year. He built a cottage on it.

In the Trust Deed of 1788 for this land it stipulated that the remaining years of the lease were vested in John Morton, yeoman. John Morton was paid fourteen pounds to transfer the Deed and land to the Trustees of the Chapel. This first building is now used as a Nursery and After-School Club.

In 1785, the Rev John Meldrum, a Scotsman who had preached in Malton for ten years, came to the Chapel. It is thought that he drew the plans for a manse for the Minister but he left in January 1786 after only 6 months and went to Hatherlow in Cheshire, where he stayed for twenty-eight years.

There is a story that he rented a croft near the Church which has been called Scotty Croft, and the nearby well has been called Scotty Well ever since. It seems a little strange that he had so much influence after only a six month sojourn in Rastrick.

The Rev Meldrum was succeeded by the Rev. Samuel Lowell who stayed for three years during which time the congregation increased and the Rev. Lowell had managed to raise enough money to get the Chapel out of debt.

The new Church experienced some turbulent years before it became thoroughly established. The next Minister started off well but then neglected his duties. After he left another minister was appointed and he alienated most of the congregation who left and met in each other's houses for services.

In 1810 a new minister, the Rev. Joseph Hemas Crisp, was appointed and he worked hard to restore services in the Chapel and to re-unite the congregation.

In 1818 while The Rev. Crisp was the Minister, George William Frederick Osborne, Duke of Leeds, sold 7660 square feet of land with the Chapel and dwelling house to the Chapel trustees for £300.

1821 – A new Sunday School was built to accommodate 150 children. It was extended in 1832 to make room for more children.

1854 – A new Chapel was built and opened in 1855. The ground floor seated 460 adults; the galleries seated 295 adults and 320 children. Later it had central heating and gas lighting. The old Chapel was sold to Mr. Charles Brook who had it moved to Brighouse where it was used as a Chapel.

The old Pulpit[5]

Ladies in the Church who organised teas and ran stalls.

[5] Courtesy West Yorkshire Archives ref. BEC:3/1093 and BEC:3/871

1878 – Work began on a new purpose built Sunday School with 12 classrooms and two large assembly rooms in the centre.

Thursday 16 March 1887 The Church took advantage of Queen Victoria's Jubilee and held a Jubilee Exhibition, on behalf of the Funds for the Chapel, comprising Art, Industrial and Miscellaneous Exhibits and a Sale of Works. It was an ambitious and successful endeavour.

During the Second World War, the buildings were taken over by the Army and much damage was done, from which the Church finances never fully recovered.

April 1976 It was announced that due to continuing financial difficulties and following discussions with the district and provincial authorities of the United Reformed Church, the Church members had agreed to close Bridge End Church after 198 years and that they would move to other local churches of their individual choice.

2007-9 - The Church has been converted into apartments. The adjacent Sunday school building, having become the Sugden Memorial Hall, has had a chequered career since the closure of the Church, with a variety of uses and is currently a tropical fish emporium.

The original Church and school building is now Bridge End Nursery and Out-of School Club.

Most of the cemetery is now covered over for a car park at the side of the Sunday school, though one gravestone has been uncovered. Behind the Sunday School building and between it and the former Church are a few remaining gravestones. These have now been photographed and the inscriptions copied.

Bridge End Independent Church c 1910

Bridge End Church Converted to Apartments

White Horse Inn, 46, Rastrick Common

For many years this was a beerhouse with only one room available as a pub.
The building was called White Horse Buildings and in 1871 was occupied by 5 families. In 1881 it was occupied by 3 separate families, 2 of whom had boarders.

1871 – James Cardwell.

1877 – James Cardwell is named in the Post office Directory as landlord.

1881 – Sarah Cardwell, widow. She moved out of the White Horse into Carlton Buildings next door before 1891. Sarah died in February 1895.

1891 – John Henry Dixon Berry was the landlord and had been a wiredrawer in 1881. He and his wife Emma had 7 children. His wife died in 1895 and John died on 19th April 1898 a week before Sarah Elizabeth Berry, his eldest daughter, married Sydney Milner. In his Will he left £1028 18 3d and probate was granted to Sarah Elizabeth Berry and Robert Pearson, stone merchant.

1901 – Alfred Briggs.

Pre-1910 – Abraham Langley had married Maria Charity née Quarmby, widow of Arthur Charity, on 19th May 1902 when he was a silk dresser. When did he take over the pub? He died on 23rd. April 1910. He left £114 11s in his Will.

1911 – Maria Langley aged 52, widow.
Living with her were her nephew and his wife and 5 children. He was a miner.

1970 – Derek and Sue Maddocks. They later moved to the Round Hill Inn in Clough Lane.

The sign for the White Horse is still hanging from the building. Although very faded, it is just possible to make out the name of the pub and also the horse standing on its hind legs.

The White Horse Inn, Rastrick Common

Thornhill Road and the Square, Rastrick

The earlier photo of Thornhill Road looking downhill as though going down towards Brighouse, was taken in 1928 and on the right hand side shows a tall narrow house which could have been part of the Square. The houses in the Square have mostly been demolished but traces of their outline can be seen on one of the remaining buildings. The terrace houses on the left hand side of the road have all been sandblasted and modernised.

Looking down Castle Hill in Thornhill Road in 1928

Looking down Castle Hill in 2011

The origins of the cottages in The Square are unclear.

Were some of these cottages the ones Joseph Berry built or were they encroachment cottages?

Encroachment cottages were built on land taken from the Common or from the waste land in the jurisdiction of the Lord of the Manor. There were customary rules for such cottages. First the land should have been used as a garden or orchard. Bricks for their building/chimney etc had, prior to the building, to be burnt on the land. The house had to be built between Dawn and Dusk on the same day, the roof had to be on and a hearth and chimney had to have been built. A fire had to be lit in the hearth with smoke coming out of the chimney by dusk on that day. If these conditions were met, the lord of the manor could charge rent but could not order the cottages to be demolished.

The secret was to build these in June and organise family, relatives and friends to help! In 1768 Joseph Berry of Elland a maltster built three cottages at Castle Hill

Three more photographs of houses in the square.

and in 1768 these were tenanted by Nathaniel Berry, Thomas Travis and Elizabeth Gill, a widow. That same year Joseph mortgaged them to Abraham Crowther of Cromwell Bottom. Unable to repay the money or the interest, in 1777 Joseph handed the cottages over to Abraham Crowther. Eight years later Abraham married Sarah Inman, a widow. In 1794, after Abraham had died, Sarah mortgaged the cottages to Robert Parker for £60 at which time two of the cottages were tenanted by Joseph Dawson and William Rushworth. The agreement was that she would pay five pounds per year until the £60 and the interest had been paid off. However, four years later, Robert Parker died and in 1800 his Executors accepted payment of the remainder of the £60, and the interest from Sarah Crowther, and handed over the Deeds.[6]

The Grocer's Shop at 85, Thornhill Road, Rastrick

Various people held the leasehold for the land on which this shop was built. The land was sold leasehold by William Capel Clarke Thornhill to Edward Kitchen and Joseph Adamson in 1874. Joseph handed over the remainder of his lease to Edward Kitchen in 1874 for a small consideration. When Edward died in 1877, his widow sold the land and handed over the remainder of the lease to Ellis Whiteley who took out a mortgage so he could build on it. In 1896, Whiteley of New North Road, Rastrick, sold the buildings to William Moses, grocer, and the remainder of the 999 year lease was transferred.

1898 - William Moses sold the land that Joseph Adamson had sold to Edward Kitchen to Richard Whitaker & Sons, Ltd., Brewers, for which he was paid £800. Directors of this firm held the lease from 1912 – 1925 (Joseph Whitaker) and then from 1925 to 1944 (George Murgatroyd Whitaker). The shop was rented out for many years.

1908 – Herbert Squire, grocer and beer retailer was the tenant. He moved to Greetland where he was manager of a grocery store in 1911. He and his wife Annie had 6 surviving children. He died in 1959.

Joseph Henry Dixon and his wife Lily Ann Dixon took over the tenancy from Herbert Squire but didn't stay long before they moved to a grocer's shop at 4, Closes Road, Rastrick.

1911 – before this census**,** Annie had taken over the shop at 85, Thornhill Road from the Dixons. Mrs. Simms' husband Albert had died in 1908. He was born and brought up in Brighouse and became a silk dresser. He moved to Galgate in Lancashire for work and married Annie Calverley in 1883.[7] They lived there for some years, during which time Harry and John were born. The family then moved to Brighouse and they lived in West Street, where Herbert, Annie and James were born. They were married 28 years and had had 6 children all but one of whom lived to adulthood. Only four of Annie's children moved with her, Harry having married Alice Eveline Maude in September 1908.

---

[6] Yorkshire Archaeological Society Ref: MD286

[7] Marriage certificate in Parish Register for Galgate, held by Lancashire Record Office.

Her son John, originally a joiner but by this time a grocer, married Hilda Willey in 1912. She died in 1919 and in 1921 he married a widow, Mabel Thornton and they lived in Mount Pellon, Halifax where John had a grocer's shop.

This old photo shows Mrs. Annie Simms standing in the door way of the shop at 85, Thornhill Road. The young man is her assistant and is probably her third son, Herbert Simms, who worked with her in 1911.

Above the door the sign announces:-
Annie Simms Grocer & Provision Dealer.
Licensed Dealer of Ale and Porter Off the Premises. Tobacco.

Her son James entered the business as you can see in his marriage certificate in 1935.[8]

Page 185.

Any Correctional Notes must be written in this margin.

1935. Marriage solemnized at the Parish Church in the Parish of Brighouse in the County of York

No.	When Married.	Name and Surname.	Age.	Condition.	Rank or Profession.	Residence at the time of Marriage.	Father's Name and Surname.	Rank or Profession of Father.
369	July 2nd	James Simms	31	Bachelor	Grocer	85 Thornhill Road Rastrick	Albert Simms (Deceased)	Warehouse man
	1935	Alice Lister	27	Spinster	—	"Glenwood" Woodhouse Lane Rastrick	Sam Lister	Baker

Married in the Parish Church according to the Rites and Ceremonies of the Church of England by after Banns by me,

This Marriage was solemnized between us, James Simms, Alice Lister; in the Presence of us, Herbert Simms, Winifred Mary Simms; [illegible] Vicar of Brighouse

1935. Marriage solemnized at the Parish Church in the Parish of Brighouse in the County of York

No.	When Married.	Name and Surname.	Age.	Condition.	Rank or Profession.	Residence at the time of Marriage.	Father's Name and Surname.	Rank or Profession of Father.
370	July 6th	Walter Hudson	25	Bachelor	Dyers Labourer	79 Bridge End Rastrick	William Hudson	Shoe finisher
	1935	Rose King	32	Spinster	Worsted twister	13, Spring Street Brighouse	Tom King (Deceased)	Engineer

Married in the Parish Church according to the Rites and Ceremonies of the Church of England by after Banns by me,

This Marriage was solemnized between us, Walter Hudson, Rose King; in the Presence of us, Frank Hudson, Jane King P King; F. W. Cop Assistant curate.

[8] By permission of West Yorkshire Archives

Annie is listed in several Trade Directories, including one issued in 1936, as running the shop and holding the off-licence. Annie died in 1943 and a year later Richard Whitaker & Sons Ltd., sold the premises to Annie's son James and his wife Alice. In the Deeds, James is a Grocer and Licensed Victualler. They installed a bathroom in the premises.

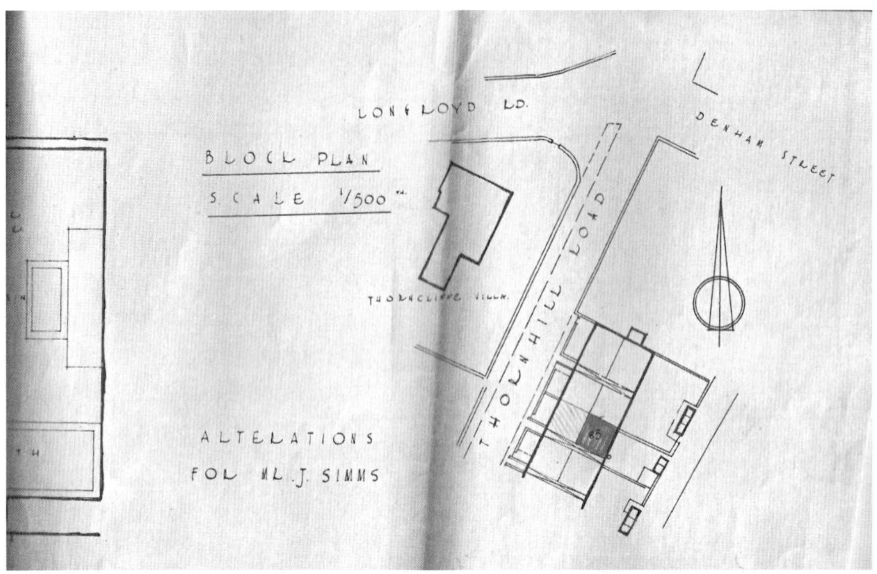

Proposed alterations at Simms grocers shop, 85, Thornhill Road, Rastrick, Brighouse[9].

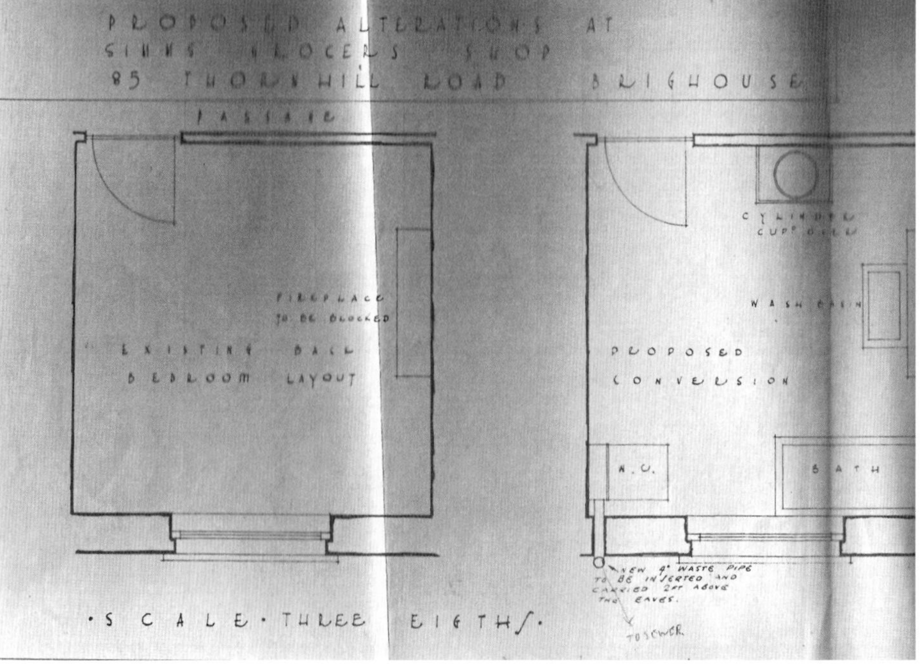

[9] With the permission of Mrs. Ives.

They continued to own the business but in 1953 his sister Annie Simms must have had some interest in the business as she had a retailer's Off Licence. Nine months later, she transferred this licence to her brother James.

James' wife died in 1957 and he continued to run the business until October 1980 when he sold it to Gordon and Jennifer Bird. They sold it and transferred the lease to Gordon Lupton and Veronica Helme the following Spring. Oddly enough Albert and Annie Simms had their niece living with them in 1891 and 1901 who was called Elizabeth Helme, born in Galgate, Lancashire. Was this another connection?

James died in late Autumn 1981.

The Helmes soon sold the shop to Dennis Charles and June Wimbles.

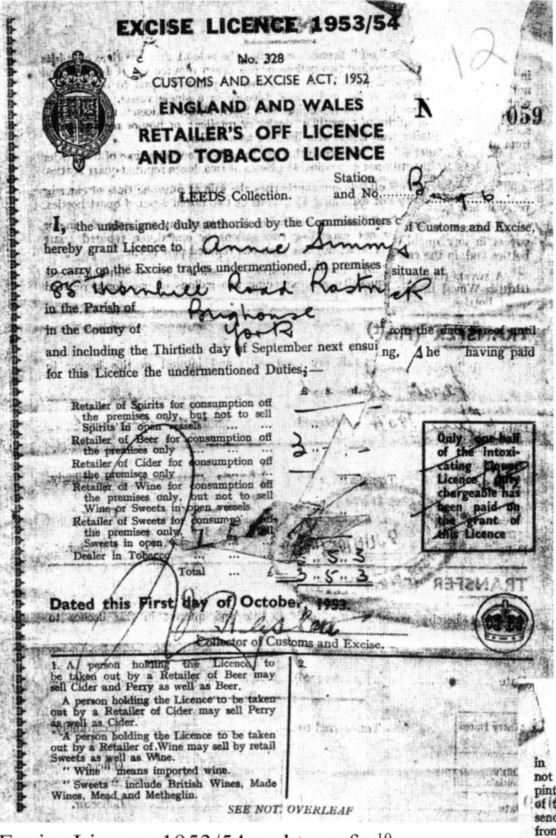

EXCISE LICENCE 1953/54

No. 328

CUSTOMS AND EXCISE ACT, 1952

ENGLAND AND WALES

RETAILER'S OFF LICENCE AND TOBACCO LICENCE

059

LEEDS Collection. Station and No. B 6

I, the undersigned, duly authorised by the Commissioners of Customs and Excise, hereby grant Licence to Annie Simms to carry on the Excise trades undermentioned, in premises situate at 85 Thornhill Road Rastrick in the Parish of Brighouse in the County of York from the date hereof until and including the Thirtieth day of September next ensuing, he having paid for this Licence the undermentioned Duties;—

	£ s. d.
Retailer of Spirits for consumption off the premises only, but not to sell Spirits in open vessels	
Retailer of Beer for consumption off the premises only	3
Retailer of Cider for consumption off the premises only	
Retailer of Wine for consumption off the premises only, but not to sell Wine or Sweets in open vessels	
Retailer of Sweets for consumption off the premises only, ... Sweets in open ...	
Dealer in Tobacco	5 3
Total ...	£3 5 3

Only one-half of the Intoxicating Liquor Licence duty chargeable has been paid on the grant of this Licence

Dated this First day of October, 1953.

Collector of Customs and Excise.

1. A person holding the Licence to be taken out by a Retailer of Beer may sell Cider and Perry as well as Beer.

A person holding the Licence to be taken out by a Retailer of Cider may sell Perry as well as Cider.

A person holding the Licence to be taken out by a Retailer of Wine may sell by retail Sweets as well as Wine.

"Wine" means imported wine.

"Sweets" include British Wines, Made Wines, Mead and Metheglin.

SEE NOTE OVERLEAF

Excise Licence 1953/54 and transfer[10]

NOTE

...r's "off" licence authorises the sale at any one time of spirits not exceeding two gallons or one dozen reputed quart bottles, and ... reputed quart bottle other than a quantity equal to one reputed ... is sold under a Justices' Licence in a single vessel. The holder, unless he is also the holder of a Spirit Dealer's Licence must not sell ... spirits to a rectifier, dealer or retailer; or buy or receive spirits ... retailer who is not also licensed as a dealer.

...ailer's "off" licence authorises the sale at any one time of beer, cider ... quantity not exceeding 4½ gallons or two dozen reputed quart bottles.

...ler's "off" licence authorises the sale at any one time of cider or perry in any quantity not exceeding 4½ gallons or two dozen reputed quart bottles.

A wine retailer's "off" licence authorises the sale at any one time of wine or sweets in any quantity not exceeding two gallons or one dozen reputed quart bottles and, in the case of wine, not less than one reputed pint bottle.

A sweets retailer's "off" licence authorises the sale at any one time of sweets (British Wines) in any quantity, not exceeding two gallons or one dozen reputed quart bottles.

TRANSFER (First)

I hereby transfer all my right, title and interest in this licence to James Simms

Date 4 June 1954 (Signed) Annie Simms

Entry Dated 3.6.54

Transferred to James Simms accordingly.

Offr's Initials ... Officer.

Date ... Collector.

9 JUN 1954

TRANSFER

I hereby transfer all my right, title and interest in this licence to ...

Date ... (Signed) ...

Entry Dated ... Transferred to ... accordingly.

Offr's Initials ... Officer.

Date ... Collector.

[10] With permission of Mrs. Ives

In 1985 Mr and Mrs Wimbles sold it to Mr. and Mrs. McHale and in the process this communication was sent:-

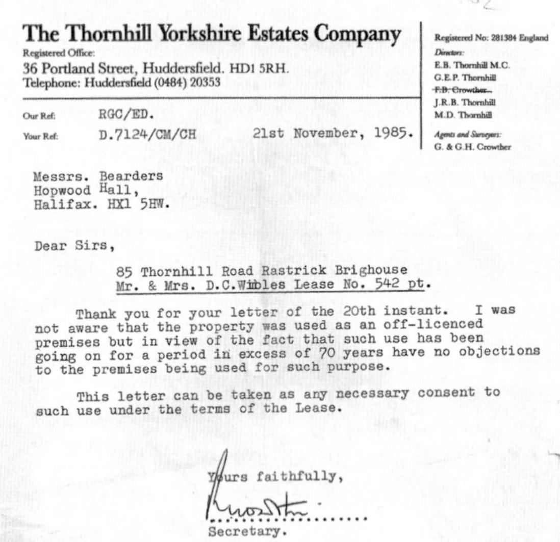

The Thornhill Yorkshire Estates Company

Registered Office:
36 Portland Street, Huddersfield. HD1 5RH.
Telephone: Huddersfield (0484) 20353

Registered No: 281384 England
Directors:
E.B. Thornhill M.C.
G.E.P. Thornhill
~~F.B. Crowther~~
J.R.B. Thornhill
M.D. Thornhill
Agents and Surveyors:
G. & G.H. Crowther

Our Ref: RGC/ED.
Your Ref: D.7124/CM/CH 21st November, 1985.

Messrs. Bearders
Hopwood Hall,
Halifax. HX1 5HW.

Dear Sirs,

85 Thornhill Road Rastrick Brighouse
Mr. & Mrs. D.C.Wimbles Lease No. 542 pt.

Thank you for your letter of the 20th instant. I was not aware that the property was used as an off-licenced premises but in view of the fact that such use has been going on for a period in excess of 70 years have no objections to the premises being used for such purpose.

This letter can be taken as any necessary consent to such use under the terms of the Lease.

Yours faithfully,

Secretary.

Thornhill Yorkshire Estates Company[11]

In 1986 it was sold again. It remained a shop with the same owners until it was closed in 1998 and converted into a private house. It still has the lintel over the downstairs window, the only house in the road to have this.

85, Thornhill Road is now a private house

[11] With permission of Mrs. Ives.

Rastrick Grammar School.

There are records of tuition being available in Rastrick long before John Hanson bought some land and meadow called Southedge (or Southage) and some other land called Wellclose and bequeathed it in 1621 in his Will to his son and sons-in-law, with the condition that they should use some of the rental income for the maintenance of Divine Service in St. Matthew's and the teaching of a school there.

Most tuition was done by the local clergymen as they were, in general, poorly paid. There is a record of a schoolmaster in Rastrick in 1548 and Robert Ramsden, who acquired the Chapel of Rastrick when it was suppressed with the passing of the Chantry Act of Edward VI, taught his nephew, Sir John Savile during the latter years of Edward's reign.[12]

After the Chapel was rebuilt and re-opened in 1603, the village had no money to pay a curate. They appealed for permission to take in four acres of land from the wastes and common "to converte the same to and for the use and benefitte of such person…..as should celebrate divine service and keepe a Schole in the said Chappelle for their better maintenance thereof" and this was granted in June 1605. John Hanson's legacy in 1621 supplemented this. Presumably the school continued to be held in the Chapel. It would be available only to children of parents who could pay the Curate for their tuition.

Mary Law, who was John Hanson's great-granddaughter bequeathed money for a charity for poor widows and also endowed a school in Rastrick " for the teaching and instruction of twenty poor children to read and write". These two charities were separate but were managed by the same trustees until 1874. Between the proving of Mary Law's Will and 1743, there is no record of such a school. In 1743 and 1746, curates of the Chapel sent returns to their Archbishop in York stating that there was no school for the teaching of poor children.

In 1777, Joshua Holroyd was appointed school master of the English Charity School in Rastrick by the Archbishop of York. This meant that no Latin would be taught. He also acted as Clerk to the Township of Rastrick. He was still in post in April 1792.

A year later, James West, clergyman was appointed master of the school. By 1801 he had persuaded the trustees to open a subscription list to raise funds. The total amount raised was £137 11 shillings. Further money was raised by selling off some items from the old school and by selling stone, possibly quarried from land bequeathed to the school, bringing the total to £206 16 shillings and 1¼d. Amazingly enough that was exactly what the new school cost to build and it was opened before May 1804.

Joseph Wrigley was James West's Usher and following the latter's death was appointed schoolmaster. He was also a land surveyor and excelled at calligraphy.

The twenty poor scholars were still taught to read and write but could also learn arithmetic if a small fee was paid. Wrigley extended the syllabus when he took over in 1822 and other pupils could study "Reading, Writing, Arithmetic and English Grammar; Bookkeeping, mensuration of superfices and solids, land-surveying, algebra,

[12] Journal of the Yorkshire Archaeological Society Vol. XVpp421-2

trigonometry and geometry and geography with use of the globes" for the weekly cost of three shillings and threepence. By 1833 he was teaching 51 boys and one girl.
After his death in 1848, there was a succession of Schoolmasters of short duration.
In 1875, the school was recognised as a Grammar School and remained as such until it was transferred to Rastrick High School.
Some years ago, the empty building was bought and became an Independent School, retaining the name Rastrick Grammar School, although it is now Rastrick Independent School.

The top of Thornhill Road with cottages and a glimpse of the old Rastrick Grammar School 1913

The now privately owned independent school in the former Grammar School has taken over several of these houses

Brighouse & District Industrial Society Ltd.

Branches:- **Church Street, Oaks Green, Castle Hill and Bridge End, Rastrick.**

An early attempt was made to open a store in Church Street Rastrick in March 1857. A man called Wright Robinson was appointed to run it. Soon after the store was opened, he arrived at the shop one morning and found there had been a burglary and goods worth £14.10s had been stolen. The store closed after only four months of trading. How much the burglary influenced the decision to close the shop is not given. A store was built and opened in Castle Hill and we do have a photo of that in its hey day but it is no longer in existence.

Castle Hill Coop Store

Another purpose built store was opened much later at the junction of Church Street and Thornhill Road, Rastrick. Unfortunately we have no photo of it in its early days but just the remaining items in the next two photographs.

The Church Street, Rastrick Cooperative Store building

The draper's section

31 January 1981 – The Brighouse Cooperative Society's Church Street branch in Rastrick closed. Many residents were worried that they would not be able to buy fresh food daily. They made several objections against the decision of the West Yorkshire Cooperative Society to transfer the business to either Field Lane, Rastrick, store or the King Street store in Brighouse.

Oaks Green Industrial Cooperative Society Branch.

The first shop here opened in 1861 in the premises owned by John Sykes, Tailor. In the financial period from December 1860 and May 1861 the sales at this shop amounted to £537.

1864 - Title Deeds for the land for the new Co-operative Store in Oaks Green were signed and George Carr Jessop was one of the signatories. He was born in 1834 and in 1857, when he married, he was a fancy Woollen weaver living in New Hey Road, Rastrick. He was one of the early Co-operators and in 1863 he had been a founder member of the Upper Edge Baptist Church and one of the first two deacons there. He became a grocer and draper when the newly-formed Brighouse & District Industrial Society opened a branch at Bailiff Bridge. From there he moved to the new Branch in Wyke in 1872. Within 5 years he had moved to Attercliffe-cum-Darnell near Sheffield where he was again manager of a new branch of a Cooperative Society. He was also a founder member of the Baptist Church there. His three sons followed him into the Cooperative stores as assistant grocers. The eldest, Turner Jessop moved to Greys' Thurrock, Essex, where he became Secretary of the Cooperative Society and later Secretary of the new Cooperative Bank. The others became store managers.

Henry Bentley was a shopkeeper in Oaks Green between 1841 and 1860. In the 1861 census he is described as being a Grocer in Oaks Green. There was mention elsewhere of his having been employed by the early Cooperative store as shopkeeper but that reference has not yet been verified.

Oaks Green Branch of the Cooperative Store in 1913

Oaks Green Cooperative store

The former Cooperative store is now a wholesale and retail Millinery business

Bridge End Cooperative Store

The Bridge End store was opened in August 1872 and Albert Pilling, who had worked at the central store, became the manager.

September 1872 - An Abattoir was opened at the Bridge End Branch which served all the stores for fifteen years. John Lancaster was the first manager.

Bridge End Cooperative store

Looking down Bridge End at the Cooperative store

Facing the Bridge End Cooperative store

The abbatoir was at the back of the Bridge End Cooperative store

Thornhill Arms

John Thomas Armitage was the Innkeeper prior to 1841 and continued to be until he died in 1867. Born in 1802, John Thomas was a farmer of 14 acres, a butcher and Innkeeper. He married Sarah Horsfall in 1833 and they had 8 children. His daughter Mary married a butcher and after her father's death she, her husband and 5 children, came to live next door to the Thornhill Arms, presumably to help her mother. However, James Smith, Mary's sister Ellen's husband took over the Thornhill Arms.
1867 – 1881 – **James Smith** married Ellen in 1864 and he is described as an Innkeeper and farmer. In 1865 he is described on their son George's baptism record as being a butcher but in 1869 and 1870 on their other sons' baptismal records, he is an Innkeeper but, of course, there is no Inn named. In 1871 they have three children:- George, born in 1865, Arthur born in 1869, and John William, who was 8 months old at the time of the Census.
Thomas Bottomley Dyson took over the pub in 1877.
The Inn was large and they held various meetings and special events there and here are two examples:-
In the second week in Dec 1877 the Annual Dinner of the Lodge of the Ancient Order of Druids was held in the Lodge room. 132 members and widows of former members attended and it was reported in the Huddersfield Chronicle that the dinner was much enjoyed.[13] Afterwards the election of officers took place.
On 22nd Dec 1877 – they held a **Knurr and Spell event** in the evening. A supper was given to 9 couples of Knurr and Spell players. On the following day they engaged in a friendly game of Knurr and Spell.[14]
At some time before 1881, James and Ellen Smith left the Thornhill Arms and moved to a farm in Oakes Green where they had a farm of 67 acres and he employed three men.
Thomas Bottomley Dyson was the licensee in 1881 and until his death in 1896. Thomas was a mason builder in 1861 and living at Greenhead, Oakes Green and was still there in 1871. He married Elizabeth Sykes and they had a daughter and two sons, one of whom died at about a year old. Thomas is described in the 1881 census as a Licensed Victualler at Thornhill Arms and that he was farming 14 acres. He died in 1896.
By 1897, **Elizabeth Dyson** is the licensee.
1901 – **Mrs. Elizabeth Dyson**, aged 65. After her husband died in 1896, Elizabeth continued to run the Thornhill Arms. Her son Frank ran the farm of 14 acres as her husband had. She is running the Thornhill Arms. Maud Mary Fieldhouse is employed as a domestic servant. Maud and her brother Harry were brought up by Elizabeth's daughter Ellen and her husband Francis John Whatmough when they were running the Stott Arms in Hipperholme. They were described as cousins, but I have not yet found the family connection. Mrs. Elizabeth Dyson continues as licensee and appears as that in the 1911 Census. Elizabeth died on the 1st September 1911 aged seventy-five years. Her son was granted letters of administration of her Will. The personal effects were valued at under £300.

[13] Huddersfield Chronicle
[14] Huddersfield Chronicle

In 1917 the licensee was **James E. Lumb** and the man standing outside the pub in the photograph is thought to be him. As this shows the tramlines the photo must have been taken after 1923 when the line was opened so, if this is James, he followed the tradition set by his predecessors of staying at the Thornhill Arms for many years.

Thornhill Arms with the licensee James Lumb outside it.
Taken after 1923 as the tram service started that year

2011 The Thornhill Arms eventually became a residential home which closed in 2012

1936 - 7 – **H. Sanders** was the licensee when the pub closed. After it closed as a public house, it was altered and turned into flats. It remained flats until some years after the end of World War II but eventually the premises were converted into a residential home for the elderly and in 2012 it was closed.

The Saxon Cross at St. Matthew's Church.

The Saxon Cross, which stood upon this base, is described in a document recording the restoration and rebuilding of St. Matthew's Chapel in 1602. The writer said "And theer stood in the Street nye to the Chappell door one crosse of stone verye fynelaye graven with frettid worcke." (sic) It is a scheduled Ancient Monument and dates from the 9th century.

Saxon Cross base taken in 1912

Hanna del Crosse (people often took their name from where they lived or what they did) is mentioned in the Manorial Court Rolls of 1285 because he held one acre and one perch of land and also shared another half of an oxgang with John, son of Richard.

In 1314 Henry de la Croix died and his son Peter paid 40d as a heriot on 5 acres with buildings. Henry seems to have prospered. A few months later Peter sold the 5 acres of land to William de Rastrick for 40 shillings – a fortune!

Sadly the cross has disappeared – possibly a victim of the Commonwealth era. The earlier photo was taken in 1912.

The more modern one was taken in 2011. What was the original purpose for the white building in the background?

Saxon Cross base 2011

St. Matthew's Church, Rastrick

Early records dating from the fourteenth century show that a Chapel stood in Rastrick and that Church fell into disuse during the troubled times of the Reformation. It was illegally sold to Robert Ramsden who used it as a stable and barn. After an Act of 1597 it was returned to the parish. It was in such bad repair that it was rebuilt between 1602 and 1605 by the villagers and local landowners. There are several documents describing in detail the contributions of building materials, days' work with horse and cart and days' labour by local landowners and the villagers during the rebuilding of this Chapel. It was re-dedicated and by 1607, the Vicar of Halifax led a service and recommended the singing of the Choir. The present Church replaced that one and opened for worship in 1796.

Later there are lists of subscribers towards the cost of a Church bell and even later the cost of the clock "the better for the good of the villagers so they could be on time" (presumably for work) but in the period of Luddite troubles, the faulty chiming of the clock saved a man from hanging.

The present clock at St. Matthew's Church topped by a weather vane

St. Matthew's Church Gallery with pews dating from early 19th century

Alterations since it was built have also been the work of local people and include the replacement in 1879 of the old pews in the main body of the Church and under floor heating and flagstones. The original pews remained in the gallery.

During these repairs and restorations, a stained glass window was fitted in the East end. The window in the South side was placed in memory of the Rev. Thomas Hayne who was the incumbent of Rastrick for over thirty years. The new pews, together with the original ones in the gallery, could seat 800 persons. Nowadays, the Church can safely and comfortably seat about 300.

It is an unusual design for an Anglican Church but lends itself very well to being a fully integrated Anglican and Methodist Church which status it has held since the 1970s.

The photographer who took the earlier photo in 1885 had an interested audience. The photographer in 2011 aroused only passing interest. Sadly the stone work has been affected by the emissions from local chimneys between 1885 and the passing of the Clean Air Acts of the 1960s.

St. Matthew's Church in 1885 from the top of Jumble Dyke

The same view 127 years later

The two early views of the interior show some minor changes between the taking of the first one and that of the second. Comparing the modern photo with those, one can see what a tremendous improvement the removal of the door and internal walls (to the left of where the pulpit used to be) has made. The insertion of another stained glass window there has not only enhanced the appearance of the Church, but allows far more light into the Church.

Interior of St. Matthew's Church[15]

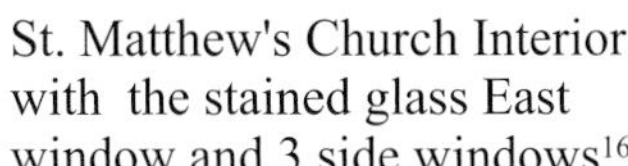

St. Matthew's Church Interior with the stained glass East window and 3 side windows[16]

St. Matthew's Church interior with 4 windows in side aisles 2011

[15] By kind permission of the Vicar

[16] Courtesy of the Vicar

St. Matthew's Church almost hidden behind the Upper George Inn and cottages in 1924

This view of St. Matthew's Church is almost totally obscured by the huddle of cottages. There is no date on the photo – nor is there a weather vane.

According to the Census of 1901, Number 1 Church Street was the Thornhill Arms. Edward Booth, caretaker for the Constitution Club, lived at number 3; the next house was uninhabited and the one next to that was number 11 in which lived Joseph Hall, steel wire drawer, and his 7 children, among whom were a costumier, a school-mistress, a joiner, a photographic artist and a scholar. There were two shops: Abraham Sykes was a Grocery dealer and his wife Hannah, who was a baker, lived at number 13 and next to them, at number 15, was Samuel Broadbent, a cabinet-maker.[17] Were some of these cottages the ones in this old photo? Was it taken from the window of a nearby house?

The Upper George Inn was the first building in Crowtrees Lane and was a fairly large Inn which was demolished in 1936 and eventually replaced by a car park.

Did the Church plant the trees to obscure the Inn? If so they did a thorough job because they now obscure the Church from the car park!

The Upper George and the cottages were replaced by a car park

[17] Census of 1901 ref: RG13/4117 with thanks to the National Archives

Upper George Inn, Crowtrees Lane, Rastrick.

1822 – *Thomas Aspinall Snr*
1834 – Joseph Shaw
1845 – William Chambers[18]
1847 - Joseph Marshall
1851 – John Fox, born in 1813, was the Innkeeper and his mother, Hannah Fox who was born in 1782 was also involved in running the Inn. She was widowed in 1836 and continued to run her late husband's carpentry business, employing one man, and the 17 acre farm, for which she employed one man. Her unmarried daughter, Hannah who was a milliner and dressmaker also lived there. Her widowed son James' daughter, Nancy Mary Fox, also lived there.
John was unmarried and was a carpenter and the Innkeeper. He died in January 1859. James, his brother, took over the licence.
1861 – 1869 James Fox was not only the innkeeper but is described in the Trade Directory of 1863-4 as farmer, brickmaker, builder and timber merchant.
In 1841 James Fox was a carpenter living in Fixby. He married Ann Dearden (called Nancy) in 1834. They had 5 children but Nancy died when giving birth to the fifth. Their second son died in infancy and their fifth child was brought up by her grandmother in Church Street, Rastrick.
By 1851 James is a timber merchant and his surviving children, Joseph, Hannah and Sarah are living with him in Shepherd House, Fixby.
1859 He married Susanna Thornton on 30 June at St. John the Baptist Church, Halifax. In that year he also took over the licence for the Upper George Inn.
His son Joseph married Ann Armitage, daughter of John Thomas Armitage, Licensee of the Thornhill Arms, and they were living at the Upper George Inn with their new baby, James Armitage Fox.
Joseph is in business with his father as a timber merchant.
1869 - James Fox died and his widow, Susanna, moved to Little Woodhouse where she lived alone until her death in 1878. She is buried in the same grave as her husband, his first wife and his mother.
Joseph, his wife and children moved to Castle Hill where he continued in business as a timber merchant. Ann died in 1874 and Joseph in 1877. Their eldest son and daughter moved to Delf Hill and brought up their 4 younger brothers and sisters. James Armitage Fox carried on the Timber business and later they all moved away.
1871 – 1877 - George Dyson (also Contractor and farmer) was the Innkeeper. He and his wife and 2 of their adult children lived there and they had 3 lodgers and a boarder. George was the uncle of John Exley Dyson at the Star Inn.
John Exley Dyson and Joah Pearson of the Globe Inn were executors of George's Will when he died on 27th October, 1877. Effects were under £450.
1878– William Sutcliffe and his wife, Elizabeth, had run the Duke of York Inn at Bridge End before moving to the Upper George Inn. William died in January 1879.

---

[18] 1845 Walker's Trade Directory

1881 – **Mrs. Elizabeth Sutcliffe**, widow, was the Licensed Victualler and her 17 year old daughter Emma assisted her.

1889 – Frederick Sykes took over the licence.

1891 – **Mrs. Elizabeth Sykes**, widow of Frederick Sykes, continued to run the pub.

1897 – Sam Collins took over the pub.

1901 – **Sam Collins**

1906 – **Jos. Morton**

1908 – **Fred Ormerod**

1936 – **Mrs.Liz Huggett** was the licensee when the pub closed. This Pub closed in 1936 and was demolished. There is now a car park on the site.

The Upper George Inn, Crowtrees Lane

A Car park replaced the Upper George Inn

Crowtrees Lane, Rastrick.

This early photograph was taken long before the road was modernised when this section was left as a quieter access way to the buildings and houses there.
At the top of this section stood Crowtrees Free Methodist Chapel with a thriving Sunday School and Scout and Guide groups. In this photograph, looking down Crowtrees Lane, the Chapel railings and gates are shown but there are no houses next to the Chapel.

Crowtrees Lane with the Chapel gates on the left but no new houses next to the Chapel

In the next early photograph (undated) and looking up Crowtrees Lane they are newly built and the Chapel is clearly shown.

Crowtrees Lane looking up the hill, showing the Free Methodist Chapel and the new houses

Unfortunately the building in the 1970s was pronounced unsafe and was closed. The members of this Church were invited to share the facilities at St. Matthew's Parish Church. This worked well for some time and gradually the sharing increased and eventually the two Churches became The Anglican and Methodist Church of St. Matthew, Rastrick.

The modern photos show those two houses but the unsafe Church building has been demolished and two bungalows and a shop built in its place. The photograph looking down Crowtrees Lane shows the alteration to the road and the removal of the wall on the right hand side. This gives us a glimpse of the modern road and of the more modern houses on the far side of it. Most of these road improvements were made to facilitate the construction of the tramway which opened in 1923. Trams don't like too many bends in the road.

Crowtrees Lane in 2011. Bungalows and shops have replaced the Chapel

2011 No sign of the Chapel but there are houses dating from the 1920s and 1930s

These photos, sadly, were not taken at a point where the Library was visible. The Library was built in 1912 at the instigation of Alderman William Smith and at his expense. Mr. J. W. Clay gave the land which was then part of the Crowtrees House estate. He stipulated that on completion the Library should be maintained by the local Corporation. The area of land donated was 2,250 square yards and because of the fall of the land it was possible to build a house for the Librarian beneath the main Library building at the rear of it. There was a garden at the back for the Librarian and a pleasure garden at the front for the enjoyment of the people of Rastrick.
Very sensibly, Alderman Smith not only paid for the building and furnishings of the Library, but also gave £50 to provide books to fill the shelves.

The Entrance and Gates to Rastrick Cemetery.

Entrance gates to Rastrick Cemetery probably 1906

This is an early photo of the gates to Rastrick Cemetery. The cemetery was consecrated by the Bishop of Ripon on 20th August 1884. Sufficient time has elapsed for the climber on the Superintendent's house and the nearby bushes to grow to a respectable height before the photo was taken. Two further indications of time having passed are the motorised vehicle just passing the gate as the photographer took the photograph and the presence of cranes and quarrying equipment in the Southage Fields on the opposite side of Carr Green Lane. The lease for quarrying by stone mining on that site was not signed until 1899.
There are some very interesting monuments within the cemetery grounds including some poignant ones.

Entrance to Rastrick Cemetery 2011

One of the clauses in the lease for the mining of stone was that the field had to be restored to be fit for agriculture (it had been farmland before it was leased for stone mining). Those drawing up that lease had not visualised the changes that would have taken place while the stone was being extracted. The land was certainly restored to grassland but it is partly used for sport and recreation and a modern school has been built on some of it.

Pre-fabricated Houses at Chapel Croft, Crowtrees Lane, Rastrick

In the middle ground of this photograph, taken between 1947 and 1953, are the pre-fabricated houses at Chapel Croft, Crowtrees, Rastrick. In the foreground, are the workings of Bentley & Smith's Mining Quarries at Southage, Rastrick. One resident, a child in 1947, remembers the excitement of moving in to one of the houses in Chapel Croft where there was a "proper bathroom and a lovely kitchen."
At the end of World War II there was a severe shortage of housing because few houses had been built during the conflict, so even in this area which had escaped most bomb damage there was an urgent need for temporary housing. The following are taken from the Council minutes:-

July 1945 – the Housing Committee decided to erect 100 temporary homes on Council owned land. The first site of 50 such homes will be at Whinney Hill and the second will be at Crowtrees, Rastrick. Architects have been appointed and as soon as they receive plans for the houses, they will begin the work.
It was decided by the Housing Committee that the temporary Housing Estate at Crowtrees be named "Chapel Croft".

14 December 1946 – At last after several postponed deliveries, the first batch of 93 prefabricated houses arrived. Lorries brought the first two houses to the Crowtrees site. By noon on Sunday the first one was complete and was visited and inspected by several interested people. For many they were very attractive, having indoor plumbing and sanitation and bathroom. The kitchen, too, was streamlined and modern.

Looking down from Toothill Bank onto Stone mines in Southage fields
with the Prefab houses in Chapel Croft 1947

2011 Looking down from Toothill Bank - the stone mines and prefabs have gone
but Carr Green School is there

Long before 2011, when the second photograph was taken, the quarries had been worked out and the land restored, as the lease had required, and most traces of half a century of industry had disappeared. The temporary housing had also vanished and the modern Carr Green School had been built.

The Greyhound

This pub was owned by Richard Whitaker & Sons, Brewers in Halifax, who also owned The Sun Inn and Round Hill Inn in Rastrick.

***1899** – Tom Firth*

1901. **Francis John Whatmough** (4 December 1856 – 3 June 1904) who played seven matches for Yorkshire County Cricket Club between 1878 and 1882. He had also played for England. Whatmough was a right arm fast round arm bowler. He married Ellen Dyson, daughter of John Bottomley Dyson, landlord of the Thornhill Arms, Rastrick in 1882. On the marriage certificate his employment is given as a journeyman painter, which he had probably followed when not playing cricket. They were at the Stott's Arms Public House in Hipperholme in 1891. There were two young cousins living with them, Maud Mary and Harry Fieldhouse. Later Maud Mary Fieldhouse was employed at the Thornhill Arms by Ellen's widowed mother.

1904 – Francis John Whatmough died in June of cancer of the liver[19] and his widow was granted administration of his estate. The personal effects were £106.

1904 – **Ellen Whatmough**, widow.

1905 – Ellen Holmes, formerly Whatmough née Dyson. Ellen married William Holmes, a gardener.

1911 – **Ellen Holmes**, widow.

1926 – J.E.Lumb

The Greyhound Inn with a new sign about 1911

The Greyhound Inn 2012

[19] Death certificate registered 3rd June 1904.

1968 – 1989 – John Normanton

In recent years there have been many landlords, including:-

July 2011 – Sandra Craven

Nov 2011- Martin Conway

2012 – **Brian Johnson** took over the Greyhound Inn on 1st February and has decorated throughout and placed a very popular seat on the pavement outside the entrance door.

The Greyhound Inn about 1906

The Greyhound Inn 2011

An Excursion!

Interior of the Greyhound Inn in 2012

Delf Hill and Tofts Grove, Rastrick

The early photo of Delf Hill dates from 1906. The cottage on the right in the foreground was, we have been told, a fish shop. The house and wall standing on the triangle at the fork in the road have been demolished but a signpost still stands there pointing the direction of Huddersfield, Elland, Leeds and Bradford.

Delf Hill looking down to Tofts Grove

Delf Hill looking down towards Tofts Grove 2011

In 2011 it proved impossible to take a photo from exactly the same place because of the trees planted in the gardens of modern bungalows built in what was the foreground of the early photo. However, the houses and cottages are still there but they and their gardens and trees are a century older.

Tofts Grove in 1906

Tofts Grove from almost the same point 2011

The Black Horse Pub,.

This beerhouse was on New Hey Road, Rastrick, opposite the Sun Inn.
Edwin and Ann Grace Bottomley lived in New Hey Road, Rastrick in 1871. They lived next door to Edwin's widowed Mother, Leah Bottomley, who ran a grocer's shop.
Edwin is described as a stone mason. There is no mention of the Black Horse Inn in that census. Their three children are named in that Census:- Ann Bottomley aged 5 years, Jim aged 2 years and John William aged 1 year. Sadly Ann and John William died in May. Ann was buried on 20th May and John William on 24th May. There was probably an outbreak of an infectious disease as 14 children died in Rastrick between May 14th and June 1st in 1871. Jim, however, survived.
By 1881 They are living in the same place, next door to Edwin's mother, and it is now The Black Horse Inn. Jim is twelve years old and a scholar.
The building was sold in 1885 and described as a pub with a brew house and outbuildings consisting of approximately 330 square yards. The sitting tenant was Edwin Bottomley and he paid a rent of £15 18 shillings per year.
1891 – Edwin Bottomley and Ann Grace Bottomley. Edwin was a stone mason and in 1889 is described as being a builder. Ann probably ran the pub, which was common practice. Jim is now a stone mason too. Edwin died on 6th May 1891 and probate was granted to Ann on 27th July 1891. Edwin's personal effects were valued at £126 8 shillings. Ann took over the pub.

Rastrick Spice formerly the Black Horse Fisheries and originally the Black Horse Inn

1901 – Ann Grace Bottomley
1911 – Ann Grace Bottomley is now aged 75 years. She died on 30th September 1911 after having held the license for 20 years. Her son, Jim Bottomley, publican and Licensed Victualler of the Star Inn, was granted probate. She left effects of £865.
1911-1912 – Jim Bottomley took over the licence.
1913 - Thomas Rayner was the Licensee until it closed in 1913.
It closed in 1913 as a pub and later opened as the Black Horse Fisheries.
2011 - it became an Indian Take Away shop.

The Sun Inn

The Sun Inn is over 200 years old and has a well under it. Apparently, in the latter part of the twentieth century, someone scuba dived down into it to see what was there. Treasure? Apparently a pair of glasses - >>> Just 2 glasses or a pair of spectacles wasn't specified – how ambiguous is that!

The further back one goes into the history of this pub, the more difficult it becomes to distinguish fact from fiction. Written records show that in 1822 **John Bell Junior** was the innkeeper and that from 1829 to 1834 the "incumbent" was called **George Holroyd**. After 1834 there seems to be only one possible innkeeper as the name of **Thomas Hinchliffe** is the innkeeper there in 1845[20]. By 1851 **Henry Holroyd** is installed as innkeeper and he continues to be 'Mine Host' until 1866. His name also appears in the UK Poll Book and Electoral Roll in 1859 and the census records for 1851 and 1861. He and his wife had two children, George and Mary Hannah. After Henry's death, at the age of 38, in 1866, Martha, his widow and their children moved into a small cottage near the Sun Inn.
Joseph Crowther became the licensee in 1867.[21]
According to the 1871 census **Joseph Crowther** and his wife had 6 children. They left the Inn a few years later and by 1881 he is well established as a china dealer in Commercial Street Brighouse. By 1891 he is also a cab proprietor. It seems likely from details in the Census of 1891 that he owned the cab but his son James drove it and looked after the horses. He died in 1895 aged 60. He left effects worth £199 15s. His son James took over the Cab business.
The next publican to be in charge of The Sun was **Jonas Bottomley**. He took over in 1877 and was still there in 1881.
In **1885** – **Ed. Barnes, Worsted Spinners'** workpeople met in the afternoon of Saturday 10th January for tea at the Sun and had an enjoyable evening with entertainment.
Mr. Bottomley's tenure was fairly short because he had moved out soon after that and

[20] Walker's Trade Directory 1845
[21] Kelly's Trade Directory 1867

in 1889 he died at Albert Place on 12 November aged 43. He was described in the Probate record as a hotel keeper living at Albert Place, Brighouse. He left £612 5s 8d and his widow was sole executrix.

1891 – **Oliver Clegg** appears in the census as the innkeeper and Victualler. He was a butcher in Fixby and married Ann Firth in 1872. She was the daughter of James Firth, an innkeeper and farmer of 18 acres in Elland Edge, although previously he had been a stone delver and later he traded as a stone merchant.

Oliver died on Jan 21 1896. Letters of administration were granted to his wife. He left £344. His widow took over the licence.[22]

1897 – Ann Clegg married Frederick Firth (apparently not related) in Oct – Dec 1897. Frederick had had a variety of occupations one of them being assistant gamekeeper to his father at Fixby Hall. Ann died on 6 April 1898 of Typhoid Fever, her son Walter Clegg was there when she died.[23] Her second husband was named on the death certificate as being the Licensed Victualler of the pub. Probate of her Will was granted to Denison Robinson, overlooker and George Firth, Innkeeper who was her brother. Effects were £563 10s 5d.

There was a lot of publicity about typhoid fever and its causes and effects in the latter half of the 19th century. One has to ask oneself how much effect this had on the popularity of this public house, especially in the light of the event which followed three years later.

In the 1901 Census, Frederick Firth, widower is still the Innkeeper. His parents had come to live at the Inn with him and had brought one of their grandchildren with them. Frederick's father had been an innkeeper before he turned his hand to game-keeping. Frederick died on 13 Sep 1901 having sadly committed suicide.[24] The report in the Huddersfield Chronicle published on 21st September 1901 reads as follows: "At an Inquest held at the Sun Inn, Rastrick, on Saturday 14th May 1901 on the body of Fred Firth, landlord of the Inn, the jury returned a verdict that the deceased cut his throat with a hay scythe, but there was no evidence to show the state of his mind at the time."

Administration of his Will was granted to his father, Joseph Firth. Fred's personal effects were valued at £151 1s 6d.

1911 – James Carter b. 1868

After the building of houses on New Road or New Hey Road there were complaints about the lack of the new form of street lighting. In response to this in January 1877, the Gas and Water Committee of Rastrick Local Board recommended that there should be an additional lamp between the Sun Inn in the New Road and the letter pillar. They also decided that if the gas company would lay a main pipe along the road leading to Badger Hill as far as the footpath leading to the Spout, three lamps could be put up along a distance of 260 yards. In the photo taken of the pub with the tram

[22] Kelly's Directory 1897

[23] Death Certificate

[24] Death Certificate and inquest held 14th. September 1901.

coming up New Hey Road, which would be after 1923 when the service started, we can clearly see the gas lamp in front of the Sun Inn.

The tram coming up New Hey Road to The Sun Inn at the junction of New Hey Road and Dewsbury Road after 1923

2012 Buses have superceded the Trams in the post 1923 photo

Deliveries to the Sun Inn.

Although the Sun Inn continued to quench the thirst of local inhabitants, the licensees between 1911 and 1925 remain anonymous. Do you know any?

1925 - Frank Beard Berry. An Inventory exists from the Brewers R. Whitaker & Sons of Halifax to Frank Beard Berry the incoming tenant which itemises everything but does NOT give a monetary value. In 1937 there were some modernisation works done and in this inventory some items were crossed out in red as they were removed at this time. Ref WHA:10/1 WYAS Calderdale.

1925 until after 1937 Frank Beard Berry

19?? – 1946 Clifford Young 1946 Inventory Valued at £217 2s 9d WHA/10/[25]

1946 –1949 Harry Clare 1949 Inventory Valued at £398 5s 0d. WHA/10/

1949 – 1951 George Spencer 1951 Inventory Valued at £299 15s 5d. WHA/10/

1951 – 1953 William Eltringham Biggins

1953 Inventory Valued at £418 8s 6d. WHA/10/5/1

1953 - ???? Peter Henderson.

2012 - **Sandra Ann Craven** is the present Innkeeper.

The Sun Inn 2011

Round Hill Inn, 43-45 Clough Lane, Rastrick

This was owned by Richard Whitaker & Sons, Brewers in Halifax.

Until after 1861 Clough Lane appeared in the census records as Dewsbury Road.

1851 – Mary Ingham was the innkeeper of an Inn in this stretch of the road, other than the Clough House Inn, so it was probably this one. Her husband Samuel appears after the children in the Census form and was a woollen spinner. None of the family appears in the 1861 Census.

I have not found any mention of this Inn in the 1861 – 1891 census records.

In 1897 **Henry Kaye** is listed in a Trade Directory as being the licensee.

[25] West Yorkshire Archives all these inventories Ref. WHA/10 and WHA 10/5/1

The Roundhill Inn

The Roundhill Inn pub sign

1901 - Benjamin Cartwright
???? – 1952 John Willie Perkin 1952 Inventory Valued at £232 2s 7d
1952 – Percy Larryman

The inventory of 1952 listed all the fixtures, fittings, utensils and stock in trade of beers, stouts etc; an apportionment of the Licence and Magistrate's Certificate etc. They were summarised as:-

Fixtures and fittings	£192 15s 4d.
Wet Stock	£ 32 4s 8d
Apportionment	£ 7 2s 7d.

In the tap room was a gas pendant with inveiled incandescent triplex fitting. In the passage there was one electric shade.

In the Filling Bar there was a single gas bracket.
There was an electric lamp and shade.
In the Bar parlour there is no mention of gas lighting but there was one electric light bulb.
Alterations were made in 1953. These included 6 – 8" opal spheres complete with galleries, lampholders, tube and ceiling plates at a cost of £2 2s 6d each. The brewers took away some items during the alterations and allowed Mr. Larryman £23 6s 0d for them. They replaced the moquette on the long seats fitted around the Bar parlour and the tap room and also built a porch on the front entrance at a total cost of £200.
1970s – Mr. Maddocks
Pre 1980 – Derek and Sue Maddocks. Derek took over the pub from his father. Before he came to this Inn, Derek was landlord of the White Horse Inn in Rastrick Common.
1999 – John Swailes ran the pub for a few months and then put a manager in and returned to his previous job.
2006 – Maggie and Rick Starkey became licensees.

White Lion Inn and Clough House later Clough Inn

Did the Stage Coaches stop here after the climb from Elland?

Clough Lane with Clough House Inn on the left in 1906

1822 – Richard Hepworth – did he die in about 1836 – 37?
1837 – Jonas Wilkinson, born in 1804, is now the Innkeeper. In 1832, when he married Leah Hepworth he was a butcher. Was Leah the daughter of Richard Hepworth who was Innkeeper in 1822? One of the reasons for asking this question

2011 - Clough Lane with Clough House Inn in the distance

is that Jonas and Leah had a son born on 31st March 1837 whom they named Richard Hepworth Wilkinson.[26]

Jonas appears in the Poll Books of 1837[27] and 1841 in which his qualification to vote is that he has copyhold houses. In 1848 the Poll Book states that he is living at Clough House. In 1851 the census records Jonas as being a farmer of 44 acres, employing 2 men.

J. Horsfall Turner describes how a Jonas Wilkinson was clearing some waste ground when he came upon the remains of a Roman Road. Many people assume that it was this Jonas Wilkinson but Horsfall Turner, writing in 1893 says "more than a century ago Jonas Wilkinson, whilst reclaiming land known as Lower Hopper-take, near Slade Lane top, found his way obstructed by a paved road."[28] If this is accurate, then he was referring to a different Jonas Wilkinson.

Jonas died at the end of October 1856 and apparently did not leave a Will.

1861 – Sam Wilkinson, aged 21 years and his wife Eliza Ann lived at The White Lion. Sam is the third child of Jonas and Leah. He is described as a farmer of 38 acres employing one man. With them lived Sam's sisters Jane, aged 17, and Hannah, aged 8 years and his younger brothers, John aged 14 and Kaye aged 11 years. His mother Leah is living on her own next door but one. Richard, his older brother is married and living 4 doors away on the other side. He is no longer a butcher but a railway goods porter. By 1871 Sam is living in Northowram in Salubrity Street and is a brewer's drayman.

---

[26] Baptism record in St. Matthew's Church Register for 30th April 1837.

[27] Agbrigg and Morley Wapentake Poll Book 1837

[28] History of Brighouse. p.21, 1893 by J. Horsfall Turner

1871 – John Taylor was the Innkeeper and a farmer of 50 acres employing one man.
John Taylor was born and brought up in Oaks Green, Rastrick. In 1843 he married Ann and they had a daughter, Sarah, in 1846. In 1851 he was a fancy woollen manufacturer in partnership with another. They employed 20 men, 3 women, 5 boys and 2 girls. Ann died between 1851 and 1854 when he married Martha Say, the daughter of John Say, a corn miller. By 1861 John and Martha had a son, John William and a daughter, Emmeline. Sarah was living with them in 1861 when they lived in Oaks Green and he was a fancy woollen manufacturer.
1874 – John Taylor was the Innkeeper and farmer
1881 - John Taylor was still the Innkeeper and farmer with 56 acres, employing 1 man and 1 boy. John retired before 1891 and he and Martha went to live at Cross Lanes, Dewsbury Road which was next to Elder Lee.
1887 – Whatmough ???
1891- Joah Holroyd is described in the Census as Farmer and living at the Inn. He and his wife had four children and lived in Lepton until after 1885 when Annie, the fourth child, was born. He was still there in 1897.
1901 – **Robert Jagger** (also a farmer). He was born in Fixby but lived at Birkhouse farm in Clifton. He married Hannah Gooder Kirkham born in Bury, Lancashire. Her mother was Eliza Walker and her aunt Hannah Gooder Walker, both born in the Rastrick area. By 1911 Robert Jagger, cowkeeper, was living with his son Tom Kirkham Leonard Jagger in Southport, Lancashire.
1906 – **Fred Tordoff**
1908 *– Thomas Moore*
1909 – 1917 – **Samuel Clough** (also a farmer)
1919 *– ??? Egbert Marsden who is said to have gone out to pay some bills and disappeared.*
1923 *– J.W.Baker*
1923 *– Fred Mitchell*
1923 *– Godfrey S.Mitchell*
1924 *– E.Dyson*
1936 – Geoffrey Mitchell
2005 – Steve Hargreaves and Carol Dixon concentrated on the restaurant side of the business.
2010 – Martin and Lauren Cockram continue to develop the restaurant.

Rastrick's Annual Gala and Festival.

Gala Procession in Gooder Lane on its money raising way to Round Hill

Rastrick Common has changed a lot since this procession passed along the road. Long before the advent of the National Health Service, Rastrick was raising funds to support the Huddersfield Infirmary by holding a Gala and Festival every July. Every year the local cricket club hosted the event at their cricket ground at Round Hill. Some of the friendly societies and the various trades of the town marched in procession through the streets some having arranged a tableau on a cart pulled by a team of horses. This photo shows them processing up Gooder Lane and along

Changes in Gooder Lane in 2011

Rastrick Common on their way to Roundhill at the top of Rastrick. Local bands, like the Brighouse and Rastrick Temperance Band and the Brighouse Old Subscription Band, provided the music to help the marchers. Men collected money from the spectators in aid of the hospital. In the 1880s a cricket match was played on arrival at the cricket ground. There would be refreshments for sale and some athletic events. In 1881 about £36 was raised but in following years the figure was usually around £50. By 1891 the bands were also playing dance music in the evening.

4 Jun 1892 Rastrick Athletic Sports and Gala was established and they took over the arrangements and held the first combined event. The Rastrick Cricket Club had made many alterations to the ground during the previous few months.

There were 134 entries for the seven events organised by them and these included a 220 yards handicap race; a 100 yards Handicap Race (Rastrick C.C. members only); a Mile Handicap Race; a Mile Bicycle Handicap Race and a Two Miles Bicycle Handicap Race.

The sum of £30 was offered in prizes by Messrs. Fattorini of Bradford. These prizes were presented by Mr. J. Thornton of Rastrick. There were many spectators at the event who were also entertained by the Brighouse Old Subscription Brass Band at times during the afternoon. The enjoyment of the evening gala was somewhat dampened by the rain.

These Annual Galas and Athletic events continued until at least 1956 and hundreds attended in1950. The recipients for the money raised probably changed with the advent of the National Health Service.

1911: King George V's Coronation was marked in June 1911 with a whole Ox being roasted on the cricket field and an enormous bonfire being built on the top of the hill itself.

Round Hill celebrating the Coronation in 1911. This photo shows the old Vaccary stones

The vaccary stones show clearly in this photo. They date from about the 13th or 14th century and were placed to enclose grazing land for cows. The Earl de Warenne, who owned this area, was a keen advocate of improving the cattle he owned and selective breeding. These huge flagstones used for walling effectively prevented trespassing bulls!

A Gala and Sports day at Round Hill

1920s – Mr. A.C. Lane, headmaster of St. Matthew's Day school and a committee were concerned about the problems of soil erosion at Round Hill. It was decided by the Committee that Rhododenrons should be planted on Round Hill.

Another celebration Bonfire at Round Hill

1935 - The Jubilee of King George V was also celebrated.

Rastrick Carnival procession 1950

1950 - This photo shows the gala that summer.

Round Hill

The splendid prizes donated by Messrs Fattorini

Another bonfire and some people got there in good time!

The Ox selected to be the Roast!

Coronation 1911

King George V's Jubilee Fire 1935

Huddersfield Road Then and Now

Making his way down Huddersfield Road towards Brighouse, having passed the junction with Toothill Lane on the left and not yet having reached its junction with Daisy Road on the right, is the driver of this heavy duty cart pulled by 3 horses.

The road is much narrower and white lines a thing of the future. Although the early photo is undated, many years have passed judging by the current maturity of the trees in the new photo, taken in 2011.

Life was slower going downhill with a horse drawn cart but eventually they would have arrived at the bottom of the hill and plodded past the junction of Gooder Lane and Birdsroyd Lane to approach the bridge over the river as the driver of the cart in the next photo has.

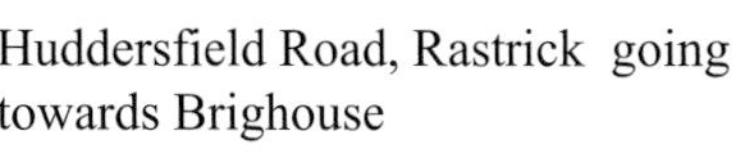

Huddersfield Road, Rastrick going towards Brighouse

The Bridge over the River Calder was widened in 1905

This early photograph was taken soon after the bridge over the River Calder was widened in 1905. On the right of the photograph at the junction with Birds Royd Lane is the one storey office of T. Smith's, a coal, coke, lime and cement merchant. The building beyond that, nearer to the bridge was, originally, the offices of the Calder Bank Mills. It stood empty for many years but about twelve years ago it was converted to a music shop.

T. Smith's office has gone but the building behind it is now R.H & G. Travis & Son Ltd., suppliers of tungsten tipped chisels.

The same junction in 2011.

The Construction of the Lancashire Yorkshire Railway

Before the railway contract was signed, the Calder and Hebble Navigation Company had been reported as planning to build a deeper waterway to Wakefield so that barges carrying 100 – 150 tons could come to Brighouse. The news that a railway was going to be built deterred the Calder & Hebble navigation from continuing their plans to expand.

The Lancashire & Yorkshire Railway Company built the railway line from Manchester to Leeds via Rastrick. The Summit tunnel from Littleborough to Walsden opened on March 1st 1841. It was 2,885 yards long under the Pennines allowing trains to travel from Rastrick and Brighouse to Normanton along the Calder Valley.

Mr. Woodward was the chief contractor for the railway East from Bradley Wood to Tag Lock in the West. He, his staff and officers and the sub-contractors made their headquarters in Brighouse and lodged in various places. Mr Woodward and his nephew Joe Bond stayed in St. Martin's Terrace. Messrs. Frank and James Wythers, who were the sub-contractors for the Lillands cutting, lodged at Miss Helm's in Lillands. The chief clerk, Mr. Tom Pierce and Mr. John Knight also lived near.

There were problems with this cutting as the bank slipped down. George Stephenson came to give advice and ordered that 3 temporary bridges be built and the earth shelved back. This cured the problem.

Temporary worksheds were erected in a small croft owned by Mrs. Waddington at the Black Swan Inn. As well as being used as workshops, these were used to store tools, equipment and materials. Hundreds of masons, navvies, carpenters and other workmen came to work on the construction of the railway and all needed accommodation for which they paid. Many families were glad of the extra money a boarder/lodger brought in. These workmen earned good money, most of which they spent in Brighouse and Rastrick, the pubs especially did a roaring trade. Two extra policemen were drafted in to support the one local policeman.

The workings aroused great interest and people from many of the villages around came to see the work being done. Every weekend people came to watch the work, lining up on the newly built bridge on Huddersfield Road.

When the cuttings were finished and Elland Tunnel had been 'pierced', the contractors held a celebration. They put seats in 12 wagons which they covered with crimson cloth. They flew flags and streamers. The wagons were drawn by horses which were decorated as if it was May Day. The drivers dressed as jockeys. The procession went from Brighouse to Elland and then on to Sowerby bridge. There they stopped for some refreshment and a rest before returning to Brighouse. When they got back there was a big dinner on the site where the goods yard was eventually built. There was a lot of champagne. Some of the rougher labourers and navvies found the store of champagne and broke the necks of the bottles and drank much of the contents before being stopped.

Photo taken of a sketch of the Brighouse & Rastrick station just after it opened in March 1841

The original station opened in March 1841 and the contractors must have left soon after as the names given above do not appear in the Census for Rastrick taken in April 1841.

The opening of the railway seemed to make little immediate difference to the creation of new jobs. There are two employees living in Lillands Lane:- Joseph Lister, aged 35 years, a railway constructor living with his wife and 3 children and Matthew Williams, aged 30 years, who is a railway porter in 1841. Another employee, Joseph Parkin aged 20 is living in Little Woodhead and he is a Railway Guard. Joseph Singleton, aged 50, is a railway agent and lived in Lillands Lane but whether he was employed by the railway or independent is not clear.

By 1895 the railway employed far more people.

People travelling to Halifax got off in Elland and those wanting Huddersfield changed at Cooper Bridge. Passengers wanting to travel to Bradford had to alight in Brighouse and go by road. A sign displayed on the platform in this early photograph instructs passengers to alight at Rastrick Station for Brighouse and Bradford. Carriages took passengers by road to Bradford.

Photo taken in 1845 of another section of the 1841 sketch

Brighouse & Rastrick Railway station in 1895

The Royal Hotel was built in 1839 to accommodate travellers. The first landlord was a Mr. Scott who also drove a coach between Rastrick and Brighouse station and Bradford for passengers wishing to go to Bradford. Goods from Rastrick and Brighouse station to surrounding places were carried by various carters including Pickfords, Chaplin and Horn, Carver & Co and several other firms. This meant that more stables were needed and temporary ones were built.

The contractor for the work at Lillands was called Mr. Green. There were already quarries in the area so some good quality stone was dug out during the excavation work. This stone was used to build the arches at Bridge End.

Between 1867 and 1871 William Morris was the stationmaster.[29] By 1877 the stationmaster was Charles Pilling[30] and in 1881 Alfred Mellor[31] held that position.

Accidents, Incidents and Diversions

Inevitably the workings attracted young boys out for adventure and mischief and at least two of them had bigger adventures than they had intended. Allan S. Avison was one of them. He and another boy were there separately and were injured on successive days, each had to have a leg amputated.

May 1898 – At 04.30 am on Saturday 14th May 1898, the driver of a light engine noticed the body of a man lying in the up-line four-foot near Longwood station and told the stationmaster. The man had probably been hit by a train as he had been decapitated and his skull and face had been badly damaged. He was taken by train and Police ambulance to the mortuary. In his pockets were 3 pawn tickets for articles pawned at Brighouse and a little money. The pawn tickets were in the name of a man in Hartshead.

Nov 1898 – Mrs Harriett H- - - - - - -, aged 76 years, travelled by train on Saturday morning from Sheffield to visit her two daughters in Halifax. It was very foggy on that day and when she reached Halifax, for some unknown reason, she crossed the line and took the train to Brighouse. There she got out of the train and seems to have got completely lost. She was found wandering in Rastrick in the late afternoon in a very confused and distressed state. Unable to give her name or those of her daughters, she was taken to Halifax Workhouse as a wandering lunatic. It was Monday before she was able to give her name and an explanation of why she had travelled to this area. On Wednesday morning she was discharged from the Workhouse into the care and custody of her daughters.

Oct. 1899 – A porter named Ernest Tidd went to check on the fire in the furnace that heated the station. The furnace was below the 'up' platform but could be inspected

---

[29] Post Office Directory 1867 and Kelly's West Riding Trade Directory1871

[30] Kelly's West Riding Trade Directory 1877

[31] Kelly's Trade Directory for Halifax and District 1881

from the room above. Mr. Tidd removed the cover and looked down into the furnace. The fire was almost 'dead' so Mr. Tidd decided to revive it. He got a can of petroleum and was about to pour some onto the smouldering mass when the can slipped from his hands.
Tremendous flames spread, burning Mr. Tidd severely about the face and head. He was immediately carried to Mr. Schofield the chemist's shop where he received temporary treatment.

28 Dec 1900 – Harry H. Hamilton's Diorama was on its way to the Rastrick & Brighouse Railway Station. Many people watched as the baby elephant "Mafek" walked along following a wagon containing a truss of hay. The keeper climbed on to the wagon to free more of the hay and Mafek seized that moment to run off. The elephant went through the top door of the station, along the covered way and through the Booking Hall, making off along Gooder Lane and over the Cliffe. The keeper and others in the company chased after Mafek and he was caught in a yard at Brighouse Fields and brought back to be safely placed in a wagon in the station.

An engine built in 1890 in Brighouse & Rastrick station in 1927

1911 – Edward Fitton was the Stationmaster and he lived at 10, Brooklyn Terrace, Gooder Lane, Rastrick.

Goods Train above Bridge End in about 1933

The South Yorkshireman

This photo was taken in 1922

Sep 1969 – The Ministry of Transport announced the closure of the Brighouse and Horbury stations after consultations and a public enquiry had been held. British Rail had proposed the withdrawal of the Manchester – York passenger service via Wakefield, Normanton, Horbury and Brighouse in July 1968 and so many people objected that the enquiry was held.
Nov 1969 - British Rail announced that Brighouse station would close on 5 January 1970.

In recent years, due to increased public pressure and a change in attitude about public transport, the line was re-opened and a new station built and opened. Compare these photos with the earlier ones.

Goods train above Bridge End in 2011 but what a difference!

The new Brighouse station in 2011

Engine Number 45407 arriving at Brighouse station in 2011

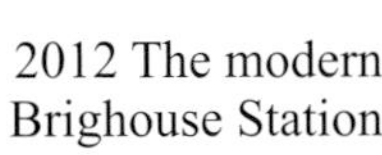

2012 The modern Brighouse Station

The Platform of the modern Brighouse station in 2012

Diesel engine the Grand Central in 2012

2011 and steam trains come through Brighouse once a week.

The new station is unmanned.

These two photographs show the present day industrial units built on the site of the old railway station and sidings.

Reinforcement on railway embankment beside the River Calder opposite Cromwell Bottom.

The Church of St. John the Divine, Gooder Lane, Rastrick

St. John's Church School. Was this originally St. John's Mission?

St. John's School in 2011

When this Church was being built, there was a keen photographer following its progress so here it is with comparison photographs taken in 2011.[32]
In the beginning:-

The building of the Church begins

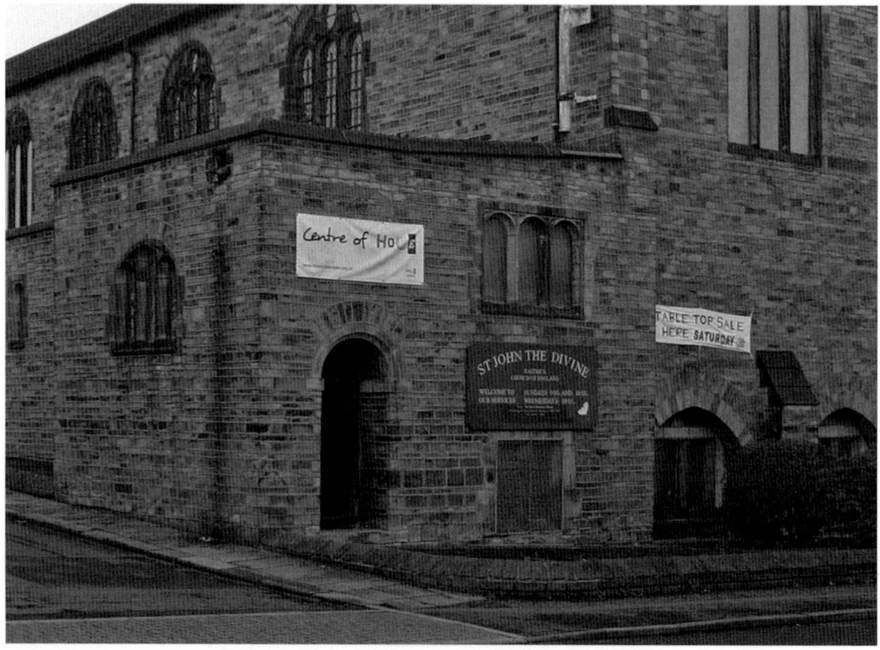

[32] We are grateful to the Church for allowing us to use their early photographs

The Foundation Stone:-

Laying the Foundation Stone for St. John's Church, Gooder Lane, Rastrick in 1912

The finished Choir Stalls

The partially built West window frame and the roof timbers

The Western end of St. John's Church being built in 1912

Looking towards the West window in 2011.

The Western end of St. John's Church in 2011

Another view of St.John's Church's interior in 2011

The east window and roof timbers

The Eastern end of St. John's Church, Rastrick under construction in 1912

The Chancel wall is being built

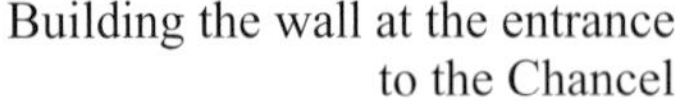

Building the wall at the entrance to the Chancel

The roof is covered in and the other half of the Chancel wall has been built.

The finished Chancel

The Chancel in 2011.

The North aisle then

and now

The South aisle

The South Aisle being built

The South Aisle in 2011

The interior of the newly finished Church

St. John's Church after 1923

And how it looks now:

St. John's Church in 2011

The Lady Chapel was completed in 1981

The Lady Chapel in 2011

The exterior:

St. John's Church and the partly finished roof

The Western exterior of St. John's Church - almost completed

The Western exterior of St. John's Church in 2011

The finished Church – note the cobbled street

the newly completed Church

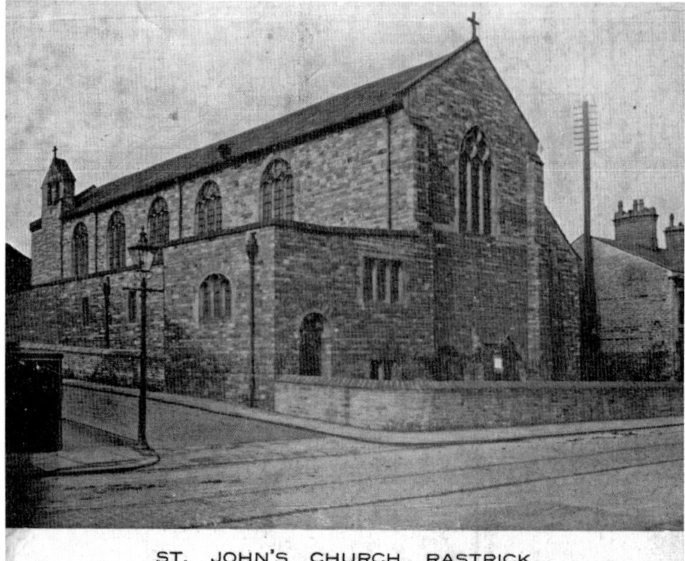

Some years after the Church was finished, this final photo was taken. It must have been after 1923 because the tramlines are there.

St. John's Church after 1923

Rosemary Lane, Rastrick

Rosemary Lane leads down from Rastrick Common into a narrow valley. This area was part of the Rosemary Park estate which was owned by John Wilkinson. Sir John Lister-Kaye inherited it and in 1773 he sold it to Dr. Joseph Fryer. The estate covered 26 acres which included fields called Scholey Hills, Far Scholey, Middle Scholey, Near Scholey and Bowling Green Bank as well as Upper Rosemary Park and Lower Rosemary Park.

Dr. Joseph Fryer was a Quaker and a stuffmaker, woollen manufacturer, apothecary and surgeon. He was in partnership with his brother Thomas as woollen manufacturers of Rastrick and London. The two brothers both died in 1816. Joseph's son Samuel died in 1802 at which time, according to Malcolm Bull's "Calderdale", he owned Bowling Green, Rosemary Mill and Rosemary Park.

Rosemary Lane in 1912

There was certainly a Dyeworks at the lower end of Rosemary Lane owned by Walshaw & Drake Ltd. The next photo shows the mill in the middle ground.

This was taken over by Bulmer & Lumb. They eventually transferred the work to the new mill they built in Bradford. Rosemary Dyeworks was demolished to make way for new houses.

View of Rastrick from Field Lane Top in 1906

Rosemary Lane in 2011

The Junction Inn, Rastrick

The Junction Inn

Built at the junction of Rastrick Common, Toothill Lane and Ogden Lane. The turnpike road called New Hey Road ran from this junction and up Ogden Lane and Crowtrees Lane to where the really new part of New Hey Road started on its journey over the hill to Denshaw, Lancashire. There used to be a mile post opposite the Parish Church giving the distances to the Junction at Denshaw, to Leeds and to Elland. There is a more modern milestone on Ogden Lane which also names the road as the Huddersfield and New Hey Road Branch Rastrick.

Landlords and Licensed Victuallers:-

1881 – James Charlesworth
1901 – Tom Thackeray
1902 – Thomas Whitaker
1906 – William Lund
1911 – Thomas Henry Hoyle
1914 – Percy Cockcroft
1923 – Jim Mornington
1925 – Albert France
1928 – Elton Greenwood
1935 – John Barley
19?? – William Clayton?
1949 – Mr. Goodwin
1950 – Arthur Walker
???? – **Donald Peaker**
1964 – Charles Rookes

1974 – David Swales. During this period, Steven Ingle, the present licensee was the first DJ at the Junction Inn.

???? - Aubrey Collins

1984 – John McGuire

1989 – Arthur Hirst

2004 – Alan and Steven Ingle. Alan is now at the Pear Tree Inn, Mirfield and Steven is still at the Junction.

Showing the meeting of Toothill Bank, Ogden Lane and Rastrick Common where the Junction Inn now is

The same junction in 2012

This photo shows the beginning of Toothill Bank on the right and Rastrick Common on the left. It has been taken from the bottom of Ogden Lane.

Trams.

The tram coming up New Hey Road from Crowtrees Lane, approaching the junction with Clough Lane was the regular service to Huddersfield from Brighouse via Rastrick, which began in 1923. The route took the tram up Gooder Lane, along Rastrick Common, up Ogden Lane, turning into Church Street past the Thornhill Arms. It continued up Crowtrees Lane and New Hey Road and turned into Clough Lane and on to Fixby and then by a private sleeper track down Lightridge Road.

The tram coming up New Hey Road to The Sun Inn at the junction of New Hey Road and Dewsbury Road after 1923

The Huddersfield tram system was started in 1881 and the first trams ran in 1882. However, the route to Brighouse was planned to be constructed in 1914 but was postponed until after the end of World War I. It was actually an extension of an existing route to Sheepridge. At first they had intended to build the tramway along Huddersfield Road and then Bradford Road direct to Brighouse.

Brighouse Borough Council considered that this would mean Rastrick and Fixby would be isolated with no transport to either Brighouse or Huddersfield. The engineers and planners realised that the existing road through Fixby was not wide enough for the planned tramway and they decided to build a private sleeper track across some fields.

Huddersfield Corporation agitated for a new Transport Act which was passed in 1920. That authorised a double track from Huddersfield as far as Crowtrees Lane and again from the railway station along Huddersfield Road and Bradford Road to the terminus at Bonegate. The Corporation discovered that costs had increased from the £48,000 in 1914 to £81,000 in 1922 and they realised that they couldn't afford to lay a double track from the outset. However, they made provision for doubling the track at a later date without disturbing the single track when this would be done. They built passing loops at strategic points along the route. They also created a new section of Crowtrees Lane to 'straighten out' a few bends!

The track was laid along Bradford Road out of Huddersfield and to the New Inn, later the Ashbrow and in June 2012 the Mumbai Spice Restaurant. There it turned left and went up the slope which was at a gradient of 1:8 and onto the purpose built private sleeper track the across the fields to Clough Lane.

Laying the drains for the sleeper tramtrack WYK 1450.2.1.7

The drains are covered for the sleeper tramtrack WYK1450.2.1.7

Work proceeds steadily WYK1450.2.1.7

Another section of the work nearing completion WYK1450.2.1.7

Completed and working WYK1450. 2.1.5

It was the responsibility of the conductor of the first tram to open the gates and that of the conductor of the last tram to close them every day.

March 1923 Watching the first tram at Carr Green on the extended track from Huddersfield to Brighouse via Fixby and Rastrick

Three thousand sleepers were used on this track and were supplied by two firms: Jarratt Pyrah and Armitage and T.W.Ward Ltd. The rails were slightly smaller than the normal size being five inches high and the base being five inches wide instead of both measurements being seven inches. This meant they weighed eight pounds less per yard. These were made by Walter Scott Ltd.

A trial run was made in January 1923 and then the whole track was inspected and approved.

It was officially opened in March 1923. The Mayors of Huddersfield and Brighouse and other officials travelled on the special tram which was decorated with 900 lamps. After that first official run, the same tram continued to run all day between Brighouse and the Sun Inn in Rastrick. Fares were charged but the proceeds were divided equally afterwards between the Huddersfield Infirmary, the chosen charity of the Mayor of Huddersfield, and to a charity chosen by the Mayor of Brighouse.

The first Saturday after that opening ceremony, the trams must have been full and busy all day. 11,358 passengers sampled the joys of tram riding and the Huddersfield Tram Company was happy to take over one hundred and forty pounds in fares.

A regular tram service must have been a boon to the people living in Rastrick. I am sure the visiting cricket teams would have rejoiced too. Before the tram service was established they would have arrived by train at Brighouse & Rastrick railway station and then had to walk from the station up to Round Hill or Badger Hill cricket grounds and THEN play the match.

The opening ceremony for the Huddersfield to Brighouse in 1923

The tram to Brighouse from Huddersfield at the end of the tramtrack

Tram coming down Clough Lane to Rastrick from Huddersfield via Fixby

Tram lines at Top of Town, Rastrick by Thornhill Arms

A tram on the specially laid sleeper track between a point near the Ash Brow Inn and Fixby

On the left at the junction of Gooder Lane and Bridge End was a junction box for the trams. It has been removed and replaced by a seat.

Trolley buses appeared in other parts of Huddersfield from 1933 but the tram service from Huddersfield to Brighouse through Rastrick continued until 29th June 1940. An official party travelled on the last tram. Special tickets were on sale on the tram which had been signed by Alderman Norman Crossley, the Mayor of Huddersfield and the money raised went towards a War Fund called "Forces Comfort Fund".

A passing point on the sleeper TrackWYK1450.2.1.5

Climbing uphill from Huddersfield to BrighouseWYK1450.2.1.8

Along the private sleeper tramtrack WYK1450.2.1.5

Another tram on the route over the fields
WYK1450.2.2.7

Tram coming up Gooder Lane. Did the cyclist get his wheel caught in the tramline?
WYK1450.2.1.8

Church Street, Rastrick
WYK1540.2.1.11

Crews and a tram at the Huddersfield depot.
WYK1450.2.1.8

Was this a minor collision?
WYK1450.2.1.7

Tram to Brighouse
WYK1450.2.1.5

Can you identify this place?
WYK1450.2.1.5

Passing the top of Bridge End
travelling down Gooder Lane
WYK.2.1.7

Where was this? WYK 1450.2.1.1

Probably on Rastrick Common
WYK1450.2.1.1

The main reason for the delay in closing this route to trams was that L.M.S. railway objected to the idea of trolley buses running over the railway bridge at Brighouse and Rastrick railway station. The route for the trolley buses was altered so they ran along Bradford Road, Bradley Bar and what was Bradley Road but is now Fixby Road and rejoined the original route at Fixby where the sleeper track ended.

Trolley buses ran until June 1955 and were, in their turn replaced by buses. The biggest drawback to trolley buses was their inability to overtake each other. So now we have motor buses which cannot overtake each other because of the rest of the traffic.

The last Trolley bus coming up Gooder Lane in July 1955

Gooder Lane - no more trolley bus wires. 2011

Trolleybus coming down Ogden Lane, Rastrick after 1940 WYK1450.2.2.6

Fare Stages on Trolley bus route from Brighouse via Rastrick to Longwood WYK1450.2.1.9

Route No.

BRIGHOUSE - LONGWOOD 90

STAGE No.																		
1																		BRIGHOUSE (Bonegate)
2	1½																	BRIDGE END
3	1½	1½																JUNCTION INN or RASTRICK POST OFFICE
4	2	1½	1½															CARR GREEN LANE
5	2½	2	1½	1½														SUN INN
6	3	2½	2	1½	1½													LIGHTRIDGE ROAD
7	3	3	2½	2	1½	1½												MARLBOROUGH ROAD
8	4	3	3	2½	2	1½	1½											LONG HILL ROAD
9	4	4	3	3	2½	2	1½	1½										SMITHY
10	5	4	4	3	3	2½	2	1½	1½									HONORIA STREET
11	5	5	4	4	3	3	2½	2	1½	1½								BEAUMONT STREET
12	5	5	5	4	4	3	3	2½	2	1½	1½							JOHN WILLIAM STREET (queue)
13	6	6	5	5	4	4	3	3	2½	2	1½	1½						OUTCOTE BANK
14	6	6	6	5	5	4	4	3	3	2½	2	1½	1½					TRIANGLE
15	7	7	6	6	5	5	4	4	3	3	2½	2	1½	1½				PADDOCK HEAD
16	7	7	7	6	6	5	5	4	4	3	3	2½	2	1½	1½			MEG LANE
17	8	8	7	7	6	6	5	5	4	4	3	3	2½	2	1½	1½		ROSE & CROWN
18	8	8	8	7	7	6	6	5	5	4	4	3	3	2½	2	1½	1½	LONGWOOD

Gooder Lane in 2012 with a modern bus

Lands House

Lands House circa 1980

This shows Lands House taken in 2012. It was the home of Alderman William Smith, Mayor of Brighouse, manufacturer and owner of Badger Hill Mills. He founded the orphanage at Boothroyd and built and furnished the Library in Rastrick. The house has been a privately run Residential Home for some years. Internally the plasterwork on friezes and ceilings has been retained. Some of these photos show the access to the tower – not for the fainthearted!

Lands House 2011

Cast iron moulding!

The original staircase but with a lift inserted!

Some of the original etched windows

The elaborate cornice in the dining-room

The tower at
Lands House

Some of the chimney pots
at Lands House

The mechanism for the now disused Dumb Waiter is still in the tower room.

The way up the tower from the tower room

Field Lane, Rastrick

Here is another example of an early colour photograph.

In 1911 there were ten cottages and houses in this part of Field Lane. Number eighteen had been divided into two dwellings; in one of which lived John and Mary Ellen Taylor and their daughter. John was a stone miner. The other part was occupied by Emma Thackray, a widow, and her four daughters.

The last house was occupied by William and Mary Ann Quarmby and their son and daughter. William was a farmer and milk seller; his son worked on the farm and his daughter worked on the milk round.

Field Lane in 2012

Throstle Nest Farm, Shepherd's Thorn Lane, Rastrick

Originally this was part of the Toothill Estate.
In 1841 Zephaniah Smith, born in 1795, and his wife Elizabeth lived here with their six children. He was a farmer. Zephaniah was born in Leeds but must have come to the Rastrick area when young as he married Elizabeth Aston in April 1827 at St. John the Baptist Church in Halifax.
There were two dwellings in Throstle Nest in 1841, the other tenant was James Hudson aged 51.

Zephaniah and his family were still there in 1851 but he was farming only 6 acres. The other tenant, whose surname is illegible in the Census records had 24 acres and employed a farm labourer. By 1861 Zephaniah had retired and he and his wife had moved to Chapel Hill, Huddersfield. He died in 1878.

When this early photo was taken around 1905, Joe Walton was the tenant farmer. In reality the farm was more of a smallholding than a farm and to supplement his income from it, Mr. Walton began to make wooden toys which he sold to local families. One of the shops in Brighouse heard of them and from then on he supplied the shop.
The farm was sold in 1918 to Cornelius Kershaw. Eventually it was abandoned and in 2011 there was only the arch of the cellar roof still left.

Throstle Nest Farm circa 1905

Remains of Throstle Nest farm in 2011

The Lady Chapel at the Church of St. John's the Divine

Chapel in St. John's Church

Chapel in St. John's Church 2011

The interior of the Church of St. John the Divine

The East windows in the Chancel of St. Matthew's Church, Rastrick in 2011